Published by One Door Press.

# ONE DOOR PRESS

Image Courtesy: Syda Productions

Malene Jorgensen – How to Become a Fashion Writer: Taking Your Writing to the Runway

ISBN-Print: 978-1-77181-006-7

ISBN-E-Book: 978-1-77181-005-0

2 | P a g e

# Disclaimer

Though the author has used her best efforts in preparing this book, she makes no representations or warranties with respect to the accuracy or overall completeness of topics covered in this book, as strategies for web content do change over time.

The advice and strategies contained herein may not be suitable for all business situations, including your own. Consult with a professional before making any changes where appropriate to better your business. This book is meant to be informative and educational at best.

Neither the author nor the publishers shall be held liable for any loss of profit or any commercial damages, including but not limited to special, incidental, consequential or other damages.

# A Note from the Author

This book is inspired by those who I often talked to at Fashion Week as I sat there, adoring all of the fashion bloggers who were scrambling to get every detail of every dress down on paper. Yes, I'm talking about those who were struggling to make rent payments because they loved fashion so much that they just had to be there – front and center. They couldn't see themselves doing anything else, but write about fashion. I hope this book will serve as inspiration to start something for yourself and grow it in the direct you see fit. I hope to be a helpful source to those who continue to sit in front row, scrambling to pay rent.

*This book is dedicated to my one and only mother – the one who always thought fashion was way cooler to write about than anything else online. I appreciate your continuous advice, encouraging me when I feel on top and believing in me when I feel down. While our fashion sense may be different at times, whether we are color blocking or adoring floral prints, we can always appreciate all things fashion. What we have taught each other when it comes to fashion is that it is much better to buy things on the spot if you know you like it, because having it shipped from an international address is way too expensive. Thank you for being my runway superstar.*

# Table of Contents

Introduction                                                13

Chapter 1: Portfolio                                        19

1.1 What is a Portfolio?                                     20

1.2 Different Portfolio Mediums                             24


Chapter 2: Creating a Website                               27

2.1 What are Niche Websites?                                30

2.2 Creating Your Website                                   33

2.3 How to Operate and Maintain Your Website               52


Chapter 3: Creating a Brand                                 57

3.1 What is a Brand?                                         58

3.2 Brand and Logo Development                              60

3.3 Maintaining the Integrity of your Brand                62

3.4 Role of Social Media in Branding                        64


Chapter 4: Go the Business Route                            69

4.1 Online Magazines and Content Mills                     70

4.2 Getting the Content and Images                         72

4.3 Understanding Monetization     73

4.4 Advertising     76

4.5 Google news and CPM     79


**Chapter 5: Contracts and Copyrights**     81

5.1 Writer Contracts     85

5.2 Understanding Copyright     88

5.3 Avoiding Lawsuits     89


**Chapter 6: Expanding Your Brand**     91

6.1 Choosing Your Direction     92

6.2 Low Budget Magazine Printing     93

6.3 Merchandise     96

6.4 Branding Expansion     99


**Chapter 7: Organization and Accounting**     101

7.1 Organization     102

7.2 Scheduling     104

7.3 Accounting     105


**Conclusion**     107

**Appendix: Sample Business Plan**     113

Executive Summary                          114

Business Description                       114

Market Strategies                          116

Competitive Analysis                       117

Design and Development Plan                118

Operations and Management Plan             119

Financial Components                       120

# Introduction

*"We are shaped and fashioned by what we love." –*
*Johann Wolfgang von Goethe*

The fashion industry is said to be one of the most competitive industries in the world. From my experience alone, people will step on you, just to get a foot in the door – even at Fashion Week. If you are not fighting for your spot, you won't get inside. This cut-throat attitude isn't just for fashion designers looking for one of the limited spots to show a collection at Fashion Week; this includes everyone who even thinks about the fashion industry. I was no designer; I was just a mere blogger, trying to get to my first fashion show, but I was nowhere near the only one struggling to make it inside this intriguing industry. Fashion models, for example, are often competing to get work and some take drastic measures to suit the demands of employers. Even designers are throwing together quirky outfits to be unique in relation to the next designer in line, wanting so desperately to get a spot on the runway. However, designers and models are not the only two groups of people who are competing for the limited spots inside the tent. Media, photographers and bloggers are all lumped together in the same group, often competing for the exposure when talking about the latest trends from runway shows.

If you feel like you are just another fashion blogger in the sea of bloggers, then you are right. It seems that every girl has a fashion blog these days, whether they attend shows or just talk about the newest trends they see in clothing stores at the local mall. Almost every girl who has a fashion blog probably strives to be involved with the fashion industry somehow, whether they are blogging about clothes, shoes or accessories. Sometimes, it can be difficult to stand out in a group of millions, especially if you are just starting out in the blogging world.

However, it isn't all about first-come first-serve when it comes to blogging about fashion. There are hundreds of bloggers out there that may have been blogging for years, but are not getting any exposure. It may be because they really have no idea what they are doing. Sure, they may know their fashion and recognize a Louis Vuitton dress when they see it, but when it comes to the online world and showing up in search engines, they may be doing all of the wrong things – or just not doing anything. Just because a blog is much older than yours doesn't mean that it will automatically do better when it comes to readers. A fashion blog must have the same operational standards as a regular blog; have a goal, meet the technical requirements set out by search engines such as Google, suit the needs of the given audience, and show consistency. If bloggers don't follow the rules, chances are that readers will find similar content elsewhere. And that 'elsewhere' could be your blog.

If you have picked up this book, chances are you either have a blog already that you want to improve, or want to start an online fashion venture from scratch. Perhaps, you want to make a career out of it. If you have a blog already, I suggest you read through this book and make a list of the changes your blog requires to make it more successful. It could be the smallest thing that is preventing you from getting success as a fashion blogger. If you are just starting out, you have a large task ahead of you. It is one thing to set up your blog; it is quite another to get the attention of readers, when there are thousands of other fashion bloggers already online. But that doesn't mean it is an impossible task. You just have to be smart about it.

Another reason why you may have picked up this book is because you have read my other book, "How to Start an Internet Business: 7 Ways to Turn Your Passion into Profit." In that book, I talk about various ways to make something profitable online, where blogging is just one of those ways. If you have read that book, you may realize that you can create various fashion ventures online. I will touch upon some of those options in this book, as I do find that some of those methods will do well when it comes to fashion. However, some of those platforms, such as an online community or podcasts, may not be as effective when talking about fashion.

Because you have picked up this book, I assume you want some useful information. I love the quote above from Johann Wolfgang von Goethe - "We are shaped and fashioned by what we love" - and I love seeing people who strive to do what they are passionate about. When people work with something they love, they will get up in the middle of the night so they can continue working and there is no such thing as a weekend. These people, including myself at times, work upwards of 7 days a week and can easily work over 15 hours per day. Sometimes, it is the family that is pulling you away from the computer or friends calling you because they haven't seen you in ages. Unfortunately, being passionate about something and investing hundreds of hours into it doesn't mean that it will make money. This is one of the most heartbreaking things I have experienced. People will work tirelessly on something, such as a fashion blog, and never really see anything happen with it. Chances are that these people are lacking some fundamental keys to take it from point A to point B.

I have written this book in hopes of giving you the ultimate guide to make money online as a fashion writer. I have written this based on my experience as an online business owner and my years as a fashion writer, where I often sat in the front row at Fashion Week, dishing out my thoughts for content websites, bloggers and news outlets. My goal is to connect the two worlds to give you a complete – and hopefully inspirational – guide for you as you start out on your online fashion writing venture. Before you start reading the book, I just want to answer the critical questions; who, what, where, when, why, and how.

**Who**: This book is written for people who want to start writing about fashion online in a professional light. This is also a book for people who want to be in complete control of where the money is coming from. If you want to be a fashion writer for a magazine, you may as well put this book down if you are preparing your resume for Glamour magazine or hoping to land a job at a newspaper that just so happens to cover Fashion Week twice a year. This book won't tell you how to get a job; this book will teach you how to create your own web business where you are in control of everything from the fashion content to your income. You can even benefit from the lessons in this book if you have a fashion blog already. You can apply the strategies explained within to make your part-time fashion blog profitable. You don't have to write fashion content on a full-time basis to get something out of this book.

**What**: So, if you don't learn how to tailor your resume for a fashion-writing job, then what will this book teach you? Well, it may actually teach you everything you need to know to get yourself noticed online. There are so many people who have a fashion blog on the web, which is something they do as a hobby on the weekends or during the major Fashion Week events around the world. Chances are that many of these blogs don't get much traffic. In fact, it is possible that some of them only get a couple of page views per month. Why is this you ask? Well, if one person is writing her commentary on Fashion Week on her blog from home as the shows are taking place, chances are that her content will drown in all of the professional websites that are actually reporting on the news, such as Glamour's website, news sources such as The Huffington Post and any successful gossip website. The question isn't so much about getting the page views immediately; it is more about how you can put your blog next to those big websites to get more attention. Usually, with more attention comes more profit.

So, let me answer the same question a little bit more directly. This book is meant to show you what you can create online that will make you a competitive online source when it comes to writing about fashion. Rather than fall into the category of being an "online fashion blogger" with the thousands of others trying to do the same as you, you will learn ways to either improve your blog or start a new profitable venture. Of course, this will take a lot of time and hard work, but the fashion world was never easy on anyone.

**Where**: The biggest question I get about what I do is whether I work from home or not. Well, if you are running your own business – and yes, running your own fashion blog full-time should be considered running a business – then it doesn't really matter where you are geographically. The "where" I want to talk about is where you will be making your money and where your content will be shared. When people think of online businesses, they often think of either eBay or an online service. Blogging has become a more profitable way to work, but there are other ways to make money online. Print and digital sales are also options. I will go into this more in the appropriate chapters.

**When**: Another question I often get is when to start your blog. If you like fashion, I'm surprised you don't have one yet. But if you don't have a blog and you have decided to go in that direction, then now is the best time. While you may feel a little lost and unmotivated writing on a website with no real direction or focus, I hope you will find some inspiration in this book, as focus is a must when it comes to online writing. Plus, when you all of a sudden decide to start working on the site on a full-time basis, you are going to regret it if you don't have any content on your site at all. In addition, there are technical advantages to getting started now rather than when you actually want to start working full time. But I will touch upon that later.

**Why**: Why would you want to be in control of your own online fashion empire and set your own schedule? Well, the "why" part is something you may be able to answer better than me. I would want to create a fashion website for all to see to let my passion become something informational and enjoyable for all of my readers. In addition, I would want the freedom to set my own hours, be in control of my own profits and run my own business. Before you actually start anything discussed in this book, it may be a good idea to answer this question for yourself; the answer may be your motivating factor as you start out on this journey.

**How**: While I have a few ideas up my sleeve as to how you can create something profitable online, it really does come down to you. I can offer you the tools and the knowledge to start exploring some of the things you can do online, but much of the actual work comes down to you. To make a blog successful, you have to invest lots of time into creating valuable content that stands out from everything else available on the same topic. To make a magazine successful, you have to do extensive marketing to make sure that readers know your magazine exists. If I show you how to create these things for yourself, will you put in the effort? If you are ready, I suggest we dive right in. Remember, you have the experience and passion. Otherwise, you wouldn't have picked up this book. It is time to sell your knowledge about the fashion industry to the fashion lovers.

# Chapter 1: Portfolio

When you look for a creative job, an employer will often ask you for your portfolio. Web developers will have portfolios with their previous work to demonstrate what they are capable of. A writer will have samples of their work, whether it has been published online or in print. An artist looking to get hired for an art project will bring samples of paintings or other artist work to showcase just what he or she is capable of. A portfolio is a broad demonstration of what a person is capable of and contains various pieces of work, depending on the industry. As a fashion writer, your portfolio will be similar to that of a writer – just with a focus on fashion.

If you are trying to get a job at a leading fashion magazine, for example, the employer interviewing you may not be willing to further the interview process if you are lacking a strong portfolio. No one really knows what you are capable of when it comes to writing. Sure, you may think you know the difference between a Louis Vuitton and a Chanel gown, but the employer doesn't know that. And it is one thing to say it; you should be showing it.

Even though you are not looking for a job or an employer to impress in this case, you should keep this mentality in mind. When you start sharing your opinions on various designers online, you have plenty of people judging your work – your readers. While you aren't trying to impress an employer, you are trying to impress your readers because your readers are those who will make your blog a success. It is a simple formula; the more readers you have, the more page views you will get. The more page views you have, the more money you could potentially make. And the more successful you are with your fashion venture, the more exposure you will get, hence invitations to major fashion events. In other words, a portfolio is a key element when starting out. If you already have an online blog, you can simply add a portfolio to your website to give it a bit more meat to showcase your talents and abilities.

The next couple of sub-chapters will describe how you can build your fashion portfolio. The chapters will define what a fashion portfolio is, how you can create a fashion portfolio, and show you different mediums you can create it in. In the second chapter, "Creating a Niche Website," I will show you how to create your own website, so if you are starting from scratch, it may be a good idea to revisit this chapter so you can get the best out of your online portfolio.

# 1.1 What is a Portfolio?

As defined above, a portfolio is a compilation of your work that best represents you as a professional individual. It doesn't matter what industry you work in; a portfolio is often the key to proving your abilities and showing potential employers or workers what you are capable of. Even though entrepreneurs don't have employers to impress during a job interview, they still create portfolios to show potential clients what they can capable of in hopes of gaining new customers or generate new leads. A portfolio has three purposes; showing off your skills and abilities, catching the interest of new potential customers, and having previous customers return because they see something new in your portfolio and trust your abilities because of previous work. For example, a dentist with an extensive portfolio of work and dental cases may find himself getting more patients because of his experience and abilities in comparison to another dentist, who is lacking a portfolio, despite being in business longer. Even though a portfolio may not be the first thing you think of when you see the successful fashion blogs online, it really does play a key component in the site's success.

The older fashion websites or magazines may not need to prove themselves and their abilities to readers. Their reputation is enough to keep readers returning every week. However, as a new writer who needs to prove abilities and knowledge, a portfolio could help establish your brand in the industry. Sometimes, building a portfolio is tiring work and for some writers, the preparation alone is a reality check for how much work is involved to work online and run a successful blog. Many think that writing one or two articles a day is enough. To really get success, you should be multiplying those numbers with 10, at least. Success doesn't come easy and writing online is no cake walk.

Now that you know what a portfolio is, you may be asking yourself how you can create one for your fashion writing, given you don't have any experience if you are just starting out. Many people will build their experience by being front row at Fashion Week, writing about anything and everything they can think of when a model is walking down the runway. However, to get into fashion shows, you have to be a part of the media or prove that you are a professional fashion writer. It is very difficult to get inside and they only let in the best of the best. Since this is a bit of a vicious cycle, the best thing you can do is build up your portfolio, get the readers, create a professional website and let your readers make you the success. Before you know it, you will have the credentials to get somewhere in the industry.

Just because you can't get in the door at Fashion Week at the moment doesn't mean you can't use the designers who are showing in your portfolio. Many other media outlets are reporting on the shows, the fashions and the designers, but none of them are sharing your point of view. To build your portfolio, you can create articles using the images readily available online for inspiration. For example, one media outlet may share a picture of the show-stopping dress at the Diane Von Furstenberg show at New York Fashion Week. The article may describe the dress in a way you disagree with. You can use the picture as inspiration for your article and write what you think about the dress, the designer, the context of the dress in the entire collection and about mass appeal. As you are building your portfolio, try to include as many different designers and countries as possible. You want to educate yourself about designers, dresses, techniques, patterns, print, accessories, shoes, runway events, models and fashion scandals that have taken place over the past couple of years. If you find that you are familiar with the big names, try to educate yourself on the up-and-coming designers who are showing at Fashion Week events around the world. Keep in mind that New York is just one of many Fashion Week events that are hosted twice a year. Other Fashion Week events include Paris, Milan, Copenhagen, Toronto and London.

When you are writing your articles for your portfolio, avoid being brief and unclear. Avoid sentences, such as "this dress is amazing" or "I want this in my closet." It seems rather juvenile and unprofessional. Those sentences are often found in the blogs written by teenagers, blogs you don't want to be associated with if you want to do this on a professional level. The golden rule for writing professionally is to take out the first-person narrative. While some people write successfully using first-person narrative, not many can pull it off. The key is to write in second-person narrative while keeping things objective.

You should aim at making positive or negative statements using descriptive and objective language. "Unfortunately, the lace feature on the arms date the piece and there are more mental associations to a grandmother's curtain than a modern fashion show," is one way to be negative in your work without using first-person narrative. Another – rather positive – example is, "the olive color of the print really suits her skin tone and it truly speaks to the masses. Chances are that this piece will be found on sale racks sooner rather than later." Here, you are injecting your own thoughts into the article without using your personal "I" to get your point across.

One reason why professional media outlets try to leave out the first person narrative is simply to make it all about the readers. If a writer continuously uses "I" in an article, it becomes all about the writer. However, an intelligent writer can easily figure out a way to share his or her perspective without actually using the letter "I" in the writing.

When crafting your articles, don't rely on a single fashion show when choosing your content. You must show your capabilities, which may include identifying specific designer traits, identifying certain techniques used by a set of designers, identifying patterns and fabrics that represent a certain era or time period, and be able to recognize the styling that went into each look. The more you can comment on the look itself, the more your article will seem comprehensive and professional. In other words, don't rely on Fashion Week shows alone.

If you plan on blogging about fashion and publishing upwards of several articles per week, the articles you are crafting for your portfolio could be used as the first articles on your website or blog. If you are planning on starting a fashion magazine, you should be using more up-to-date fashion articles unless you are writing a commentary or doing a comparison article, for example. By the time you are done your portfolio and start your magazine, several fashion shows may have taken place, dating your work tremendously. Also, keep in mind that Fashion Week operates on season, meaning the shows you see in the fall are for spring and summer the following year. Similarly, the shows you see in the spring are for the upcoming fall and winter seasons.

There is no real number of articles that will make a portfolio complete. The content should speak for itself and should show how talented you are as a writer. If you feel more confident having upwards of 20-30 articles in your portfolio to show a wide range of skills, then don't be afraid to write that many articles. Smaller portfolios may not be as convincing, as four to six articles can only show so much skill and ability. The size of your portfolio also depends on how you want to present it, which comes down to what you want to build. For example, a blog requires one type of portfolio, whereas a magazine may require another. I will touch more upon that in the next sub-chapter. In chapter 2, I'll show you how to develop a website, which can serve as your portfolio.

# 1.2 Different Portfolio Mediums

You should create your portfolio based on what type of medium you want to work with. For example, a portfolio for a magazine should look different than a portfolio for a blog, because a blog is online and free, whereas a magazine is either in print or digital with a price. While you may not be charging for your magazine, it will cost you to print the magazines for your readers. If you are planning on starting a fashion magazine, for example, you should be aware that pictures cost money and that you can't just take a picture and print it in your magazine. The picture will most likely be copyrighted and belong to the person or corporation that took the picture during a fashion event.

If you are writing about an outfit you saw online on a news website, it is highly likely that the picture was either taken by an employee of the site in question or by a professional photography distribution business, like Getty Images. Getty Images is a corporation that sells the usage rights of pictures to people who don`t have similar pictures or have the legal rights to use them. Getty has a large library of images, so you will most likely find images that suit the content you are writing. Getty photographers will attend film premieres, fashion events, red carpet events and the like to get high-quality pictures of celebrities.

Since Getty is a "usage rights" company, you have to get permission to use the photos on your website and in your portfolio. If you just take the picture without asking for permission, chances are that Getty will pursue the chance to get royalty payments from you. If you do a search online about Getty and bloggers, you will see that some bloggers have received "cease and desist" letters in the mail from Getty. Some people have even been presented with an invoice for thousands of dollars. And Getty has every right to do so; the company states clearly on the website that the content must be purchased, meaning websites have to invest in usage rights to use the images. If you do choose to invest in usage rights, you may include the picture in your portfolio. If not, then tread carefully.

You may find it easier to find pictures on social media that you can use for your portfolio. For example, a celebrity may have shared a picture online he or she snapped personally. Some social media platforms protect the rights of the photos, but many put the copyright in the hands of the users. Chances are that you will have a unique portfolio if you talk about celebrities and fashions that aren't already in the mainstream media.

When it comes to the actual content, your portfolio should show your abilities and skills as a writer. You can do this by showing a mix of anything and everything you feel is appropriate or by sharing snippets of something you have done. You want to lure the reader in and hint that you can offer much more than what the reader is seeing in your portfolio. If you are planning on running a print or digital magazine, where people have to buy access to your content, you don't want to offer too much of the content online for free. Sure, you want to give them a sneak peek at what they can expect but that can be done in snippets. If you are planning on starting or expanding on your fashion blog, you can add your portfolio to your website by simply adding a static page. I will go into more detail as to how you can add the portfolio to your website in the next chapter, as I go into details about creating your own website to get started.

If you are unfamiliar with the way a blog differs compared to a regular website, you should think about a diary. One way I can best describe it is this way; your fashion blog articles are written as "posts" which are like diary entries in your journal. A portfolio, which is a constant – or static – page on your website along with your "about" page and your "contact" page, should be created with the idea that it can be accessed at any time, despite the many updates or articles you post. Generally, the blog posts – or diary entries – will shift down on your site, meaning older content will disappear from the home page and onto archive pages. The newest article will appear at the top. However, the informational pages (about, contact, terms of use, privacy policy and other static pages) will stay put in the main menu, so readers can access this information at any time. This menu can either be found across the top of the page or in the footer.

You could create a print version of your portfolio if you are planning on running a print magazine, or if you find a need to pitch for people, whether you are looking for an investment or trying to sell advertising space for your print magazine. Ideally, you would want to have the written article right next to the image you are writing about. Purchase a binder with protective pockets, so your content is protected. Create a front cover for the first page and then dive right into the portfolio. On your left hand side of the open binder, have a picture of the content you are describing. On the right hand side, have your article pertaining to that fashion image. For every page you turn in the binder, the image of the fashion piece you are describing and your appropriate article should be visible at the same time, so the reader can reference them. You can take a few snapshots of the printed portfolio for your website if you please, but you can also simply mention that a portfolio is available upon request. If you are networking with people in hopes of getting more exposure to your magazine, it would be ideal to have the portfolio with you at all times.

# Chapter 2: Creating a Website

It seems like everyone has a website these days, whether it is a website to showcase a resume or a blog to share random content and thoughts. It seemed that just a decade ago, many websites were primary business websites or informational pages were people could go to learn valuable information. Now, it is simple to start a website, even with little-to-no knowledge of the web, coding or even writing. Many companies have created platforms where people can create a website with no knowledge of the HTML or CSS coding involved with designing a functional and interactional website.

Some of these companies offer free websites for users with an account. There is a catch to these free websites however. The company will take up advertising space on your website, which could be damning to your company or brand. For example, if you want to focus on couture dresses on your blog, the last thing you want on your website is an advertisement for weight loss or pet sitting services. The worst part about it all is that the website company is making all of the money from your readers. Sure, you get a free website but you may just be damaging your name from all of the unnecessary ads.

There are also some technological problems with using free services. The free services won't give you your own domain name. The website you are given will be an extension of the original domain – a sub-domain. For example, let's say the website company you are using the host your website is called www.freewebsites.com (this is just an example). Your domain would then become www.couturedresses.freewebsites.com. In other words, you have to share your domain with the company you are hosting with. Since it is simple to create a website these days, many people will automatically judge your abilities if your website is a sub-domain of a hosting company. For one, readers may question why you haven't invested in the actual domain.

Besides that technical requirement, there is also the issue of SEO (search engine optimization). SEO is the technique of getting your website optimized for searches, so your website will show up in search results more often than other sites when people are looking for content related to yours. SEO heavily relies on the keywords within the content, your domain and your meta-descriptions, so if you are not in full control of these key components, your website may be found on page 20 rather than page 1 of searches.

While you may feel a little overwhelmed at the moment, there are only a few things you need to think about. I will take you through it all and explain key features. The next couple of pages won't be about fashion writing as such. Instead, these chapters will teach you how to create an optimized website so you can start writing. If you already have a blog on one of these free services sites, then considering reading through this chapter to see how you can gain more control of your blog. If you are thinking about starting a magazine, whether it'd be digital or print, it would be ideal to get a website started as well, so people have a place to visit for more information.

Before we get started, you need to think about the following things;

- **Wordpress**: Wordpress is one of the world's biggest tools for creating your own website. Wordpress actually has two options for you. Wordpress.com is for people who wish to start a free blog (you will be forced to become a sub-domain website if you use the free service) and Wordpress.org is where you need to pay for your website. However, you will be gaining your own domain, which is important for branding and professionalism. If you get your own hosting service as well, you may not need to remember the two Wordpress sites, as most hosting services will link you to the appropriate website

- **Hosting**: The best way to describe hosting for beginners is the place where all of your content is stored. Your content isn't just your pictures, your articles and your design; it is everything including the Wordpress platform and domain. If you imagine a Tupperware bowl as the hosting, the food within is your content. Together, it creates a presentable and contained website. One without the other is close to useless if you want to make a career out of blogging. If you are going for the free website, you will be allowed to host your content on the Wordpress servers. However, if you plan on having more websites in your future, I suggest going with a hosting account. I will show you how to set everything up with BlueHost.com in the next chapter

- **Themes**: A theme is the basic layout of your website. Some will call it a template because it is rather simple and empty when you first install it. There are hundreds of websites online that will provide you with themes or templates for the Wordpress platform, meaning you can get your website to look the way you want. You don't have to settle for the basic theme. Themes are priced from $20 up to $50, depending on how professional they look. If the developer put much more effort into make it easier for you to navigate, expect to pay on the higher end for themes. You can browse through hundreds of themes before making your final decision

- **Plugins**: Plugins are add-ons you can download for your website. The theme you install may just offer the basic layouts of your home page, a contact page, your portfolio and your blog. You may have the freedom to change colors and layouts in terms of sidebars, but the theme may not offer much more if you are buying on the lower end. However, you can download plugins for free to make your website more professional. For example, plugins allow you to install social media buttons to make it easier for your readers to share the content they are reading, allows you to integrate a Twitter feed for your readers to follow, gives you the freedom to manage spam and advertisements, and allows you to fully customize your e-commerce shop if you wanted to integrate one of your website. So, if you feel that you don't get everything you need in a purchased theme, you may find what you are looking for in the downloadable plugins section. I will show you more about that in the next couple of chapters

Now that you understand the steps in creating your own website, you may not feel as intimidated as you did when you picked up this book. If you feel motivated to start blogging or designing your magazine, then you are showing your entrepreneurial spirits. However, before you get started on your website, let's take a look at niche websites and why narrowing your topic may help you in the end.

# 2.1 What are Niche Websites?

In my first book, "How to Start an Internet Business: 7 Ways to Turn Your Passion into Profit," I dedicated a good chunk of the book on niche blogging. The book was essentially a guide on how to make money online and niche blogging is one of the best ways to combine your passion with profitability online. The same is true with a fashion blog; it has to be niche to make good money. I have decided to use the clear definition from my first book to help you understand how "niche" works for blogging:

> "The term "niche" means that something is very focused and specific. The term has the same meaning when it comes to blogs. Niche blogs are very focused in content. A niche blog is not a blog discussing children's literature, for example. Instead, it is one that discusses young male characters in children's literature over a set period of time or one that only focuses on painted illustrations in 20th century children's literature. This is where the importance of what, where, who, why, when and how comes into play."

In other words, niche isn't just fashion in general. There is nothing specific about blogging about handbags, scarves, couture gowns and the newest in jean trends. Fashion is an industry and a topic in itself. And this is where many people get it wrong. Having a fashion blog does allow you to write about everything you find appealing within the fashion industry, but your advertisers may not find it so appealing. How would you convince a shoe store that it would be worth advertising on your blog, if only 5% of your content was on shoes? And out of all of your readers, only 3% actually read your shoe articles? It would be a hard sell. Chances are that the shoe store would much rather spend thousands of dollars on an advertising campaign for a website that only had articles about shoes, where all of the readers were interested in the shoes – not everything else happening on the site.

There are some benefits to creating a niche blog or magazine that I want to outline here. You will see them reappear throughout the book in other chapters, but I want you to understand that having a "fashion blog" with no clear direction and no focused topic will often be less profitable.

- **Advertising**: When you are searching for people or companies to advertise on your blog so you can make money on a consistent basis, companies want to find a platform to market on that reaches a certain group of people. If you are approaching a local shoe store to market on your website, they may be hesitant to invest in an advertising campaign if you are only talking about shoes 10% of the time. In other words, if you are talking about fashion in a broad sense, you may have a hard time convincing companies that they will get business from your readers. On the other hand, an accessories store may be willing to invest if your entire website is just about accessories – handbags, jewellery, hats and scarves. If 100% of your content is about items that your advertisers have available, you are more likely to get a campaign going. The same thing holds true for online advertisers, such as Google Adsense. Adsense will use keywords from your content to find relevant ads. If you are writing about everything in between gowns and scarves, Adsense may have a hard time finding appropriate ads. If you only write about shoes, the program will most likely find shoe ads

- **Expertise Status**: It is better to know everything about one area than know a little bit about everything. This is the same when it comes to fashion. It is better that you are an expert in shoes, in accessories or in haute couture than know a little bit about shoes, a little bit about accessories or a little bit about runway fashions. You cannot be a fashion expert as a blogger and cover everything that comes out of the industry. When you are trying to pitch to advertisers or trying to narrow down your target readers, it will be much easier for you to sell yourself as an expert in one area. You don't see a shoe designer creating gowns either

- **Content Creating**: The concept of "niche" is also beneficial when it comes to content creation. When you are writing an article, you have to think about advertising and building your expertise status. However, that's just two things to think about. You may find it easier to write about everything from the fashion runway rather than trying to cover everything that comes out of the industry. If you cover everything in a certain area of fashion, such as shoes or accessories, your website or magazine will have a higher chance of becoming the number one source to get information. Chances are that people will start spreading your website around using word-of-mouth advertising, meaning you don't have to do much down the road

Now that you have learned some of the benefits of having a niche blog, you should figure out what topic area you would like to explore. If you can't decide, you could do a fashion blog or magazine that talks about everything you enjoy talking about. However, you may face an uphill battle when it comes to pitching to advertisers and making money from it. You may be thinking that you can simply rely on Google Adsense, but if there isn't a strong theme throughout the website, chances are you will end up with ads that are not applicable to fashion.

When picking your niche, write down your three favourite topics within the fashion industry and see if you can come up with 20 blog post ideas for each topic. You just have to write down the title and see if you can actually think of 20 different stories for your website. The topic that you can think the most creatively about is probably the topic that will give you success. But make sure you are really passionate about it. You will be writing about this topic for a while.

# 2.2 Creating Your Website

Now that you are working on coming up with your niche topic for your fashion venture – or have it outlined already, you will need a website so you can start sharing your content. There is no better time to start a blog than now. Even if you haven't figured out your niche topic yet, you should start working on your website. If you are doing a blog, you should work on setting up and designing the website, so it is ready when you start blogging on a consistent basis.

If you are doing a magazine or another venture, it is wise to have a website as well. For example, every major fashion magazine on the market has a website that will give readers more information about the publication, information about the writers contributing information, information about applying to be featured and perhaps even a library of older issues. There was once a commercial on television that said, "If you are not online, your business doesn't exist" – or something along those lines. And I happen to agree with that statement. People always go online to search for companies, magazines and blogs, so it only makes sense that these people find your blog or magazine online rather than someone else's blog from their search.

The first thing you need to do when it comes to building a website is to find a hosting program. If you have gotten one recommended from a friend or a family member who can help you get started, I suggest you go with that. If you do have questions, you can get them answered by someone who actually uses the service on a regular basis.

But if you don't know anyone who has experience with hosting, I can only recommend the service that I use, which I have been very happy with over the past couple of years. It is also very affordable, even if you are hosting several websites on one account. I use Blue Host (www.bluehost.com), which is based in the U.S. The service also provides hosting services for Canadians. To see if the service provides hosting options for your country, email or call them to get some answers.

When you first sign up for an account, you are required to pay for the hosting required for one website. For example, your hosting may cost $80 per year. Since you are registering your website, you are buying a domain as well which is about $20 per year ($10 for the domain and $10 for the security for the domain to protect your site). In other words, for one hosting account and one domain, you will be paying around $100 per year. That is a relatively small business expensive, if you are operating from home. Every website on top of that is just the $20 fee for a domain and the protection, meaning you can host five websites on your one hosting account for about $180 per year.

Since you don't have a website when you sign up, you should have a domain name in mind. You will get the option of checking to see if it is available on various extensions, including .com, .net and .org. Since this service is U.S. based, the .ca extension is not available. For the best search results, you want to go for the .com extension, since companies often look for the .com extension. In addition, people who are finding your website by typing in the domain name in the URL address bar will often use the .com extension by default.

Once you log into your hosting account, you may be overwhelmed with all of the options available for you. You actually only need a few things to get started.

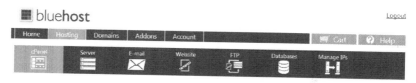

*This is the menu of your Blue Host account as of June 2013. It provides you with everything you need to build your website and more. You can even register your domain through your C-Panel and attach your purchased theme to your domain.*

When you first log into the account after registering with your email, you will see the menu above. As part of your registration, you are providing your billing address and your payment information, meaning you can start designing immediately. This is a screen shot from the summer of 2013 after Blue Host did a design upgrade. Although it may be hard to see from the screenshot, you only really need the C-Panel option, which is the first big box in the picture. It is under the C-Panel that you handle everything from setting up the website to connecting your hosting account with Wordpress.

Under the C-Panel menu, you will see several options, including "Mail," "Site Builders" which will feature Wordpress, "Files," "Domains," "Upgrades," "Promotional," "Statistics," "Security, "Databases," "Software/ Services," "Preferences," "Advanced" and "Partners." You should be worried about the "Domains" section when you are getting started. Under the "Domains" section, you have several options.

When you are starting out with your first domain, you need to register it to make your website and hosting function properly. Without your website and theme, there is nothing for you to store or "host." Your "Domain Manager" option allows you to manage all of your websites. It is under the domains registration that you can choose from different extensions as well.

Click on "Register Domain" under the "Domains" section of the C-Panel to register the domain you have chosen. I have gone through the process to show you how simple it is to get your domain registered and ready for your website.

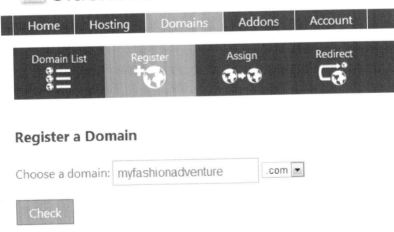

## Register a Domain

Choose a domain: myfashionadventure    .com

Check

The screenshot above shows you what you will see once you click on "Register Domain" under the "Domains" menu. I have tried to see if www.myfashionadventure.com is available for the sake of this book. If you have something creative in mind, plug it into the space available and chose the .com extension. Click "check" to see if it is available.

If you find that your chosen domain is not available, you have a few options. Of course, you could choose to buy the domain with a different extension, but you would be taken more seriously if you have the .com extension. You could try out different things, such as myfashionadventures.com instead of a singular "adventure." You could also add "the" in front of the domain name, if you are trying out fashionlover.com and it isn't available. Just because the domain isn't available doesn't mean you have to give up completely and change your niche.

*The following domains are also available. Add any domains that you would like to also register.*

| Standard Domains* | .com | .org | .net | .us | .info | .biz |
|---|---|---|---|---|---|---|
| | 14.99 | 14.99 | 14.99 | 14.99 | 14.99 | 14.99 |
| | 11.99 | 8.99 | 9.99 | 11.99 | 11.99 | 11.99 |
| myfashionadventure | ☑ | ☐ | ☐ | ☐ | | ☐ |
| TheFashionAdventure | ☐ | ☐ | ☐ | ☐ | | ☐ |
| MyFashionAdventureTravel | ☐ | ☐ | ☐ | ☐ | | ☐ |
| MyFashionAdventureOnline | ☐ | ☐ | ☐ | ☐ | | ☐ |
| MyFashionAdventureGroup | ☐ | ☐ | ☐ | ☐ | | ☐ |
| MyFashionAdventureTours | ☐ | ☐ | ☐ | ☐ | | ☐ |
| NewFashionAdventure | ☐ | ☐ | ☐ | ☐ | | ☐ |
| MyFashionAdventureInc | ☐ | ☐ | ☐ | ☐ | | ☐ |
| FreeFashionAdventure | ☐ | ☐ | ☐ | ☐ | | ☐ |
| AllFashionAdventure | ☐ | ☐ | ☐ | ☐ | | ☐ |

Show more suggestions...

This is what you will be presented with when you try to find an available domain name. Your chosen domain name will be at the top of the list and other options are listed underneath. Luckily, my domain www.myfashionadventure.com is available for registration.

Click on the domain you wish to register and follow the directions. You will just have to confirm your purchase and credit card information unless you have saved the information to your account. Once you have chosen your domain and registered it, you need to connect the dots. You have the hosting and you have the domain – now you need to connect the domain to a website you can design and you need to make sure it is all linked up to your hosting account.

Since your domain was registered through your Blue Host account, you don't need to worry about connecting your domain name with your hosting account. Instead, you need to worry about connecting your website platform (Wordpress) to your domain and to your hosting account. Luckily, Blue Host has created an installation feature that allows you to connect a Wordpress platform with your hosting account. In other words, all you have to do is to connect your domain with the platform.

To get started, go back to the C-Panel after your domain registration and scroll down until you see the "Site Builders" section. Click on the Wordpress icon. If you don't see the installation option immediately, scroll down to the "Script List" and find Wordpress under the "Blog" section. You want to click on the link that is beside the official blue Wordpress logo.

*You should see this installation option. Click on the Install option. You will then be presented with a page, where you can select the domain you want to install. Since you have only bought one domain, you should only have one option available. Click the legal agreement box and install the Wordpress platform for your website. When this process is complete, your website will be connected to both the hosting account and the domain name. You will have to repeat these steps for each domain you purchase in the future.*

Once you are done with the installation, you should check the email you have used to register your Blue Host account as the next step will be sent to your email. You will be sent some login information for your Wordpress platform. This platform is the one you will use from now on when you make changes to your website. The email you get will give you a password and a user name, which is often "admin."

To access your website, you need to go to your website with an extended "**/wp-admin**." For example, you need to visit www.myfashionadventure.com/**wp-admin**. This admin extension allows you to access your behind-the-scenes tools for your website so you can get started. You will probably find that you spend more time on the wp-admin panel than on your actual website.

*This is the common appearance of your website login page once you visit the /wp-admin page. "Admin" represents you as the website owner and the password required is in the registration e-mail. Check the domain to ensure this is the right login page for your new website. You can change the password once you log in.*

You will see the Wordpress platform once you log in. You will see a menu panel down the left-hand side. Here you have plenty of options, including creating pages, creating posts, and installing plugins. However, you need to change your password first so you can remember your password in the future. Click on the "Users" option in the vertical left-hand-side panel. Make sure you choose the "Your Profile" and then scroll down to the bottom. Right above the "Wordpress SEO Settings," you will see the password option.

Type in your new password twice and click save. You will be able to see how strong your password by checking the "Strength Indicator." If it is not strong enough, you can use upper and lower case letters and add symbols.

*This is exactly what it should look like when you are trying to set up your password. As you can see, you have the option of adding users, meaning you can register additional users under your account if you wanted to hire writers for your blog.*

Now that you have changed your password, you can start designing your website. When you register your website, you are given the standard template for Wordpress. Each year, they will issue a new free template that you can use to design your website. However, you can buy another template to really give your website that professional look.

For Wordpress themes, there is one place where you can find the most templates for your website – **themeforest.net**. You will even be able to find some that are simple enough to be used for a fashion-forward website. If you are planning on sharing lots of content, including fashion pictures, you may want to look for a simple theme, perhaps with a black and white color scheme. Many of the themes will allow you to change colors and backgrounds, so just because you don't like what you see during the preview of the theme doesn't mean it won't work for your blog. You need to look at the layout and functionality, as colors and backgrounds, link-colors and post pictures are all customizable.

You have thousands to choose from and many of them fall under $50. The more detailed or extensive templates could cost you a little more, but you don't necessarily need to purchase a theme more than $50. The themes available for this price will give you everything you need and more to really personalize your fashion blog or magazine.

If you have any questions in regards to the theme, you can go to the theme's page or the author's personal page under the themeforest.net site to see how others have rated the theme. You will also be able to see how many people have purchased the theme before you, how many comments people have left in regards to the theme and learn more about the compatibilities of the theme. For example, you can learn about the theme's compatible browsers, whether the theme has high resolution, what files you will get when you purchase it (CSS Files, JS Files, PHP Files, for example – these will all help you in the customization of the site), and whether you can add those plugins I discussed earlier.

I would suggest you browse through themeforest.net before making a final purchase. There are hundreds of themes available and most of them may suit your needs. Search different options to see what you like the best. It could save you lots of money in the end.

This is one example of a theme you can download. This is the "Sahifa" theme from TieLabs and is available through Themeforest.net. This theme will give you a featured news slider with social media icons.

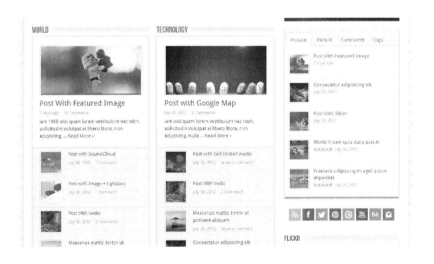

This is the same theme just further down the home page. It gives you plenty of options to have lots of fashion news and articles on the front page. Keep in mind that you can change the colors and backgrounds to make it suit your blogging vision or magazine brand.

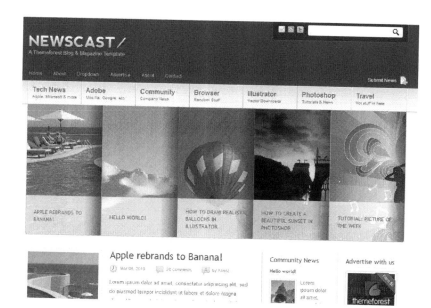

This is another theme which you can use for your blog. This gives a more interactive feel because of the accordion slider. This theme is called "News Cast" by Kriesi.

This is what the theme looks like on the front page. Again you have plenty of options when it comes to personal customization. This theme gives you plenty of content on the home page.

*You can also go for a simpler theme that allows your pictures and content to stand out more. One such theme is "Showycase" by Premitheme. This is more like a portfolio and photography theme, which is great if you can go to local shows in your community and snap those fashion pictures yourself.*

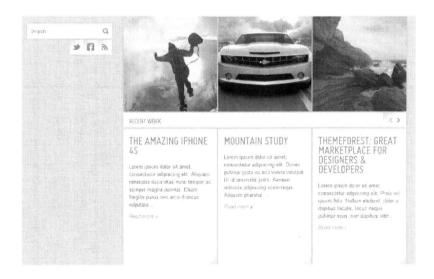

*This is what the theme looks like on the front page. Your pictures will stand out with a brief description, which is a teaser to the article.*

Once you have made a decision to purchase your theme, you need to purchase it through Themeforest.net. You can choose to buy it via your credit card or use your PayPal account to make the purchase. Either way, you will be able to download the theme immediately. Save the theme to your desktop, as it will be downloaded in a zip file. You may have to go into your "downloads" section of your themeforest.net profile to access the zip folder. You will also be given a documentation file, which explains how to set up the theme and what sizes pictures need to be for the best look, for example.

To install the theme, locate "Appearances" in the left-hand side menu of your Wordpress panel. Under here, you will find "Themes" as an option. Click on "Themes" and choose the "Install Themes" tab underneath the page's title. Select the "Upload" option to locate your downloaded zipped folder theme on your computer and wait until it uploads and installs. You are now connecting your purchased theme with your website and domain.

If you have troubles uploading your newly purchased theme to your websites, it could have something to do with the way the developer has packaged the theme. The developer may have put the zipped folder containing the theme into another zipped folder with all of the documentation you need to learn how to use the folder. If it doesn't work, locate the zipped folder and open it up. If there is another zipped folder with the same name as the theme itself within the original zipped folder, then drag this zipped folder out of the original and place it on your computer desktop. Try installing the theme now with this new folder and wait to see what happens. Refresh the website to see if the theme has worked. It will look rather plain, but you are getting a fresh canvas to work with.

You should now start designing your website and making it uniquely your own. If you do have a vision in mind for a blog or a magazine, such as a color scheme or the basic layout of your website, you can start exploring the options the theme offers. Most themes will allow you to customize your theme, meaning you can specify specific color schemes for backgrounds, panels, links and text.

If you do have a logo, you can upload it to the website as well. Your logo and blogging title should be at the top of the page on every page, so people can see what your website is called. Most themes will have a certain spot for logos and blog titles. If you don't have one, then read chapter 3.

*This is an example of a design panel that a theme may have to help you design your website. This is a panel offered by Pexeto, a theme creator I use for a couple of my websites. This panel provides you with options to customize every background, picture and link.*

This sample also allows you to customize pages and sliders. This panel is in addition to the standard Wordpress functions, so these options are there to help you make the website your own. The panel will automatically install into your Wordpress panel once you install the theme itself. You can experiment with different colors and layouts.

You should also do a copyright statement for your website. Some themes will allow you to change the copyright statement in the panel provided by the theme designer. If not, you have to go into the "Editor" section and find the "Footer" HTML code. In here, you should find a line that has the words "Copyright" and the name of the theme creator. You can take out the name of the theme creator and change the name to your own blog or magazine name.

*This is an example of a very detailed copyright statement that you will find at the bottom of your website. This particular sample is from Cosmopolitan.com. You can simple write "Copyright 2013 – name of your website. All Rights Reserved." Privacy Policy and Terms of Use can be placed under your menu or "About" page.*

You also have to personalize the name of your website and the description that shows up in search options. You may be able to do this under the panel as well. If not, then download the YOAST SEO plugin, which will allow you to do the same.

| | | |
|---|---|---|
| Site keywords | | ❓ |
| Home Page Description | | ❓ |
| Home page title | | ❓ |
| Page title separator | | ❓ |

*This is from the Pexeto theme as well and allows you to customize your title and your website's meta-description.*

**Glamour**: Fashion trends, outfits, hair, makeup, celebrity news
www.glamour.com/ ▾
Your guide to the latest fashion trends, outfit ideas, hair + makeup how-tos, and
celebrity scoop is on Glamour.com. Plus, info on this month's **Glamour magazine**.

*This is what Glamour's website looks like in a Google search. The
homepage title is "Glamour: Fashion trends, outfits, hair, makeup,
celebrity news." The keyword is "Glamour," as it appears in the
website title, the domain and the meta-description. The meta-
description, also known as the homepage description, is the section
starting with, "Your guide to the latest fashion trends..."*

Once you have taken care of the design and your copyright issues,
you can start creating those static pages. Static pages are those that never
change, no matter how much content you add over time. Examples include
"about," "contact," "contributors," "terms of use" and "privacy policy." If you
are running a magazine, you can also outline contribution requirements in
case you want people to contribute content. An example of a menu is below.

ABOUT     MAGAZINE     CONTRIBUTORS     MEET THE TEAM     MERCHANDISE     NEWS     CONTACT

*This is an example of a static menu. It can be on the top of the page
or the bottom. Some themes will allow menus on both the top and
the bottom, but it is up to you to decide what works best for your
website layout.*

When you first install your website theme, the homepage may look
rather dull. This is the page that should offer readers bits and pieces of your
information. In other words, you will need to put all of your latest news on the
homepage. You do this by changing the template of the homepage. It may
be set as the default template, but you should change it to feature the latest
news. You do this by clicking on the pages, creating a home page, and
setting the home page to the "featured" page under "template" in the
publishing option. You may have to go under "Settings" and then "Reading"
to change the "Front Page Display" to "Static Page" and then "Home."

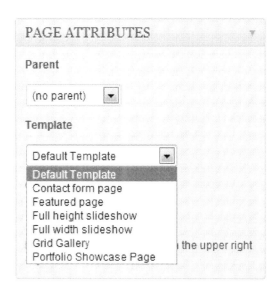

PAGE ATTRIBUTES

Parent

(no parent)

Template

Default Template

Default Template
Contact form page
Featured page
Full height slideshow
Full width slideshow
Grid Gallery
Portfolio Showcase Page

*Right under the publishing panel, you will see this. Under the "Template" option, you can set it to "Featured page" to get all of your new blogs on the home page. This drop-down menu is part of the publishing area of the pages section.*

You may quickly discover that you have options when it comes to your page layout. You can have a "full width" page, where your written content will go from one side to the other. You also have the option of implementing a sidebar that you can put on either side of the main page. The sidebar can be customized, so you can feature the content you want to share.

You can also download plugins so you can really customize your sidebars. For example, you can download a Twitter feed, a social media icon plugin and you can implement HTML code in the text box, so you can feature pictures as well. You customize the sidebars under the "Widgets" section of the Wordpress panel, where you can create several different sidebars for pages and posts.

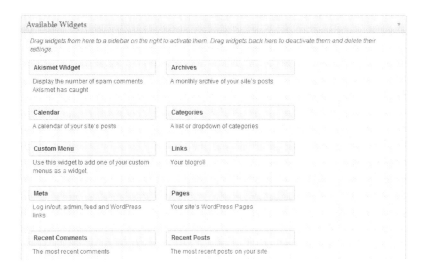

These are some of the custom widgets that come with the Wordpress theme. You can share your blog post archives so readers can sort your posts by month and year. There is also a calendar option, a categories section if you arrange your posts by categories, a recent comments option and a recent posts option. You don't have to use them if you don't find them appropriate for your website.

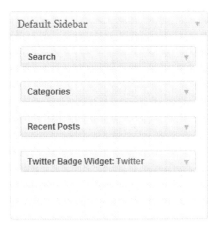

This "Default Sidebar" sample is right next to the "Available Plugins" section of the "Widgets" section. You simply drag the plugins you want in your sidebar into the default sidebar. Here, you can see a sidebar with a search bar, categories, recent posts and Twitter.

You have now created your website with your chosen theme. You have also customized the website with a copyright statement, a meta-description and learned how to make your sidebars and pages stand out. You now need to start adding your blog posts to your fashion website and learn how to maintain it as you are publishing. If you are doing a magazine, you may not want to update your website as frequently. It is up to you if you just want a couple of static pages on your magazine website or if you want to have a "news" section where you update your readers when a new issue is available, for example.

*This is an example of how a website looks when the sidebar is active. This is from my personal blogging website and you can see how the social media icons, my search bar option and my Twitter feed is in a sidebar, completely separated from my blogging content. In this example, the sidebar is on the right-hand side, but you can quickly change it to be on the left-hand side if you wish. You do this under the page in question by scrolling down to the sidebar section of the page.*

# 2.3 How to Operate and Maintain Your Website

Now that you have set up your website and learned the basic requirements to make your website more professional, it is time to focus on adding content. Content is not something you add immediately and then take a break, especially if you are a blogger. While you want to add enough content to fill up your home page, you should keep adding content on a consistent basis. You don't want to add 30 articles in the first week and then tire out completely. Your readers will be expecting new content and if you let them down, they may find another reliable blog to read. It is so easy to lose readers, so don't give them a reason to leave your blog.

If you feel very motivated one day but know that things won't be as relaxed in the upcoming weeks, you can schedule your content. In other words, if you have written 20 articles, you can space them out in terms of publishing. You don't even have to be at the computer when each post is published. The Wordpress platform allows you to schedule your work in advance, meaning you can plan out your posts for quite some time. This is called "automating posts." While you may not use this feature on a regular basis, you should use it if you plan on going out of town for vacation or just need to have a few days with no work. Your readers will be expecting to read your news, so you can schedule work ahead of time, so your readers won't notice that you are not at the computer.

Scheduling your post is a neat feature if you know that you won't have time to publish anything for the weeks to come. Chances are that you will find the tool useful on more than one occasion. While it is tempting to schedule your posts and then take a week off, I highly suggest you only schedule posts in advance if you know you can't post anything. You want to be available if news breaks, so you don't write about the event days later.

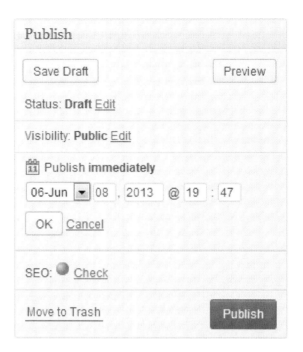

*This is how you automate your posts. In the publishing frame of your post section, you will see a publishing time. It will say "immediately." If you click "edit," you will be able to change the date and the time that the post will publish. You can do this to any post you are planning on publishing at a later date.*

Now that you know how to schedule your posts, you can essentially start writing your work. However, there are some other things you should be keeping in mind as you are working on your blog or magazine. I will cover some of these here.

- **Writing Content**: As you start crafting your articles, you should focus on bringing out the best in the fashions you are writing about. While scandals always intrigue people, you may not get the best reputation from designers, if you giving them negative attention in the media. While your readers may enjoy a little drama here or there, you may be affecting a designer's business and brand, so expect him or her to fire back at you. While you want to share your opinions on the fashion pieces or stories you are documenting, you want to think about your future relationships with the designers. Your blog or magazine shouldn't be all of your favourites, but if you want to grow your professional blog or magazine into something worth noticing, then you have to keep it positive. Designers are more likely to give exclusive interviews to magazines that have spoken fondly of them in the past. In addition, it only takes once designer to say something mean about your magazine or blog to give it a bad reputation. If fashion lovers hear a designer criticizing your blog or magazine, then your business may be hurt. There are plenty of negative people in the world who will have something to say about the designers in question. You need to think about your reputation and your professionalism.

- **Marketing**: Another thing to consider when you start publishing is marketing. You want your readers to notice your blog or magazine. While traditional marketing may cost too much on your writer's budget, you shouldn't give up marketing completely. You can use social media marketing efforts to get your blog or magazine noticed. Social media marketing involves marketing your website or magazine on popular networks, such as Facebook, Twitter, Pinterest and Instagram. You can attract new readers and followers from the networks and spread the word about your blog. If you are wondering how to get started, you can pick up several books on social media marketing. Or better yet, you can analyze how larger fashion magazines or blogs use the networks to share blog posts, magazine news or press releases. You should make it a habit to tweet, Facebook or pin something on Pinterest on a regular basis, if not daily.
- **Guest Bloggers**: As your blog or magazine grows and you get more readers, you may find yourself feeling a little overwhelmed if you want to cover all of the news in one niche area. During Fashion Week shows, you may feel overwhelmed if you are trying to cover every show possible. If possible, you can get some guest bloggers to help you out, as they will help create content for you in exchange for exposure. While some bloggers will demand a fee for an article,

others will do it for free if they can get some exposure for your website. If you do choose to get a guest blogger for your blog or a guest contributor for your magazine, make sure you create a contract for the guests to protect yourself. The content they write for you should belong to you exclusively. While the writers may have copyright over the work, the contract should state that they are only allowed to share the work with your blog. You won't be able to get readers for your blog or website if the exact same article appears on other blogs or in other magazines. This contract should be written and signed before anything is published. Also, you want to make sure that the content you are sharing on behalf of your guest is indeed their work, so run the article through a plagiarism scanner. There are several available online for free that will be able to tell you if the work has been stolen.

- **Inspiration**: While Fashion Week may be a busy time for you as designers are showing new clothing items, you may find yourself with periods of downtime when nothing is really happening in the fashion industry. To keep your readers coming back, you need to think creatively. If you find yourself looking for content, chances are you can get your creative juices flowing by taking a trip to the mall. If you are writing about styling different types of clothes, you can take a few pictures of some mannequins in the windows and offer your idea for styling. If you are writing about shoes, take a few pictures of the newest shoes on the market. It is important that you always offer something new to your readers, even if it requires more effort on your part. You may just do a simple Google search when it comes to finding new fashion stories during your downtime. However, you should be on top of everything all the time. One idea is to set up your account with some Google Alerts. Google Alerts inform you every time someone publishes something online in regards to specific topics. You can choose the keywords you want to be informed about. Examples include "fashion week," "fashions," "Louis Vuitton," "Chanel," "New York Fashion Week," "runway," "fashion designers," and so forth. You can choose keywords that fit your niche rather than cover everything in the industry. As soon as something is published, you will get an email with all of the appropriate links so you can get started on your work. If you are able to get on some mailing lists from designers or big fashion houses, it may be a good idea to do that well if it fits your topic. You don't want to share content about handbags if you are only writing about shoes. Be specific and focused, as your readers will expect nothing less.

- **Growing Readership**: Once you start getting more attention from readers, you may find yourself getting more than a thousand hits per month. You can track this via Google Analytics, something you have to set up during the early stages of your website setup. You can use these numbers to pitch to advertisers, as a company may be willing to invest in an advertising campaign on your website, if you can prove that your website for shoes gets at least 30,000 views per month. The large readership can also help you get closer to the designers you are covering. For example, a designer may be more willing to do an interview with a website or magazine that can prove some solid numbers rather than with a blog with just a few hundred readers. Even though you may feel a little discouraged in the beginning when you are getting less than 100 views per month, you should focus on the big picture. The more you write the more exposure you may get. And the more exposure you get the more designers may want to be featured. If you ever feel discouraged, compare your blog or magazine to those of the bigger websites or companies, such as Glamour or InStyle. They have been around for years and have built up a solid readership. They worked hard and it took time. Just keep trying different things, whether you are marketing your content on Twitter and sharing articles from guest writers. All of a sudden, your blog or magazine may get some serious attention.

# Chapter 3:
# Creating a Brand

Once you have created your website and start adding some content, you may notice that your logo and your website name is missing from the top of your website. Many themes will make room for a logo and a website name, because logo recognition is such an integral part of website branding. Many of the bigger fashion and beauty websites don't actually have a logo – they just use the name of the website and company as the logo itself. In other words, the name of the website is a big part of the brand itself.

In the next couple of sub-chapters, I will try to explain what a brand is and how you should start developing your own web brand from the first day. You should play around with some lettering and logo design and then be very consistent in using it on all of your business cards, website pages and social media profiles once you decide on a logo or design.

# 3.1 What is a Brand?

There have been many discussions as to what a brand really is. A brand is something that describes the entire business or website as a whole – something that connects the goal of the business with the desire of the readers. Many will argue that the brand is the emotional connection between the reader and the website – the connection that brings readers back to the website instead of going elsewhere.

In other words, the brand is something specific that the website gives to the readers. The name, the logo, the slogan and the design can all contribute to the brand. For example, the logo can help readers recognize your website from others on social media networks, which will help them connect with yours over others available on the same topic. This logo or your business name will become the main association with your website or service. Since you are writing about fashion, your logo or website name should be recognizable and should be something readers will connect with it.

There are many ways you can design your logo or website name. While you may just want to stick with the website name as your logo, you should make it stand out, so you don't use common fonts that can easily be copied or used by other websites similar to your own. Below, I have provided three examples of how bigger fashion and beauty websites have used their names as the brand rather than a logo in rather simplistic ways.

# GLAMOUR

This is the "Glamour" logo from the official website. It is bold, fuchsia and large. Because it is all capital letters, it does set itself up as an authoritative source for all things glamour and fashion. This is one example of how branding can be in the name rather than a logo.

GAMES / PROMOTIONS / FREE STUFF / NEWSLETTER

# COSMOPOLITAN

| HION | DIET/FITNESS | FOOD/COCKTAILS | CAREER/MONEY | COSMO F |
|------|--------------|----------------|--------------|---------|

"Cosmopolitan" is another example of how lettering can make the logo and branding stand out. It is similar to the "Glamour" logo, except that the pink color is a bit different. The letters are closer together and made thinner. It could resemble the big skyscrapers of New York City. This logo is also from the official website.

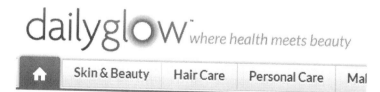

"Daily Glow" is a rather new website that deals primarily with beauty regimes and products. However, "Daily Glow" combines a little logo within the website name to make it truly unique on the website. The "O" in "glow" stands out. Whenever that specialized "O" is present, readers know that it is related to "Daily Glow."

You don't have to use the name of the website as your primary logo. You can get creative and develop something along the lines of "Daily Glow" where the logo is part of the name. You can also integrate the website' colors into your logo, as "Daily Glow" has done with dark grey, light grey and pink. Your logo is something that should represent you and your blog or magazine, so it is all up to you. Just make sure it makes an impression.

You can also choose to have a logo completely separate from your business name. In other words, your website name may be "My Fashion Adventure," where you want your logo to be a pink globe to show that your fashion adventure takes you all over the world, if you are documenting Fashion Week as your niche, for example.

# 3.2 Brand and Logo Development

If you don't have any experience with logo designs, there are plenty of sources available to help you out. One of these online resources is Vistaprint.ca, which helps small business owners develop logos and business merchandise for low prices. You can purchase a logo package for about $22, which will give you everything you need to get started on your website. They have hundreds of logos available. If you don't like any of them, you could perhaps get some inspiration as to what your logo could be.

*This is an example of the logos that are available for beauty and health-related businesses. If you are doing a niche blog on celebrity fashions and beauty, you may find one of these logos useful. If not, you can always see what you like and perhaps get some inspiration.*

If you want to design your own logo rather than buy one from a website, you can do so. After browsing around on Mercedes-Benz Fashion Week's website to get some screenshots for chapter "3.4 Role of Social Media in Branding," I stumbled across a list of their sponsors for the event. And sure enough, all of the sponsors' logos were listed for the event. Perhaps some of these logos will serve as an inspiration for your blog or website.

*These are the sponsors for Mercedes-Benz Fashion Week.*

# 3.3 Maintaining the Integrity of Your Brand

Once you have developed a logo or a business name for your blog or magazine, you should start using it on everything. Your logo or name will be on each magazine issue and it will be present on each page or post you create for your blog. It will become something people recognize instantly when browsing through articles online or searching for content on social media networks.

Because the brand and logo carry so much weight for your blog or magazine, you have to protect it. If you start analyzing some of the bigger fashion magazines or blogs, you will see that they think meticulously about everything they post, whether it is an article or a tweet on Twitter about the newest summer trends. Everything has a goal and everything can be linked back to the blog or brand in question. For example, you don't see a large fashion brand posting about the stock market news, or see an editor sharing what she had for dinner last night on the company's Twitter feed. Everything that is done in the name of the brand is done to protect the brand's goals, message and perception. Many brands represent something much bigger.

**CHANEL** ✓
9,494,343 likes · 106,270 talking about this · 14,035 were here

✓ Liked    ✿ ▼

*These are two of the logos and brands from the biggest fashion
houses in the industry, Chanel and Louis Vuitton. Both are
screenshots from their official Facebook pages. Each logo
represents something much bigger than just the name itself.*

For example, Louis Vuitton represents the newest and hottest in
leather handbags for women. Even though the fashion house now produces
dresses, accessories and everything else a woman could want, Louis Vuitton
was actually known as a leather luggage business many years ago. The
business created the best handbags and leather goods in the industry. The
LV logo doesn't just represent the monogram that really pushed Louis
Vuitton handbags into the arms of consumers. It represents the history of
French leather and high-quality goods.

The same idea applies to the mirrored Cs in the logo for Chanel.
The Chanel logo comprises two interlocked, opposed letters-C, one faced
left, one faced right. Chanel was founded by Coco Chanel by Paris, France.
The fashion house is most famously known for the cream-colored pearls with
the little black dress that has come to define Parisian fashions. Of course,
Chanel is also known for the perfume No. 5 de Chanel and the iconic Chanel
suit. The Chanel logo isn't just a presentation of the black dress with white
accent pearls – it is about the Parisian lifestyle of Coco Chanel. More
recently, the Parisian lifestyle idea has become main-stream with the popular
Chanel handbags.

The reason for providing these logos and branding stories isn't so much to give you some fashion history; it is more to show you how important and significant a brand is. It isn't just something that is used to identify a business as such. It is used to identify a lifestyle or an idea of something. If you remember back to the "Cosmopolitan" logo, which was simply the name of the magazine is tall block letters, you will understand that the logo is representing the feminine and fashionable attitude in the big city, for example.

When you are creating your logo, you should think about how your blog logo or magazine name will come across and what it will represent. Do you want to be the fashion-forward blog that talks about styling in the big city of New York? Or do you want to be the smaller Parisian fashion house that covers Fashion Week in Europe? Perhaps, you find it more appealing to sell yourself as a shoe lover who will take the e-commerce approach to sell yourself more as an online shoe store than something in high fashion. It is all up to you, but it may take time to develop this brand identity. In other words, don't feel discouraged if you don't have an identity within minutes. It could take months or even years to really establish that identity.

# 3.4 Role of Social Media in Branding

While you may have to build up your brand over several months or even years, the branding is important in several ways. The logo isn't just a representation of the history of your blog or magazine in a few years; it is also the thing that connects a marketing campaign with the product or service itself. For example, Louis Vuitton only has to show the LV logo to get instant recognition. In other words, if the LV shows up in an article or as a blog post, people know what it is about. And with that single recognition, comes the entire history as explained previously.

It is therefore important for you use the logo on everything you decide to do whether you are using an actual logo or if your blog or magazine name will serve as the logo itself, like "Glamour" and "Cosmopolitan" has done. If Louis Vuitton did a billboard advertisement for a new handbag collection, the board only had to include the picture of the handbags and the LV logo. That would be instant recognition for potential buyers. However, marketing isn't restricted to just billboards and television commercials anymore. Bloggers and small businesses will use more accessible routes, such as social media marketing.

To show how to integrate a logo and business name into your social media marketing strategy, I decided to use Mercedes-Benz Fashion Week. The Fashion Week is named after the biggest sponsor, which just so happens to be Mercedes-Benz. Even the logo for the fashion event has the Mercedes-Benz logo, even though the car business itself has nothing to do with the fashion. So, how does Mercedes-Benz Fashion Week market events and designers online without being associated with the cars?

Part of the strategy is to make the car logo a part of the Fashion Week logo, so the two become one. Then, on social media marketing sites, the car logo also stands out with the Fashion Week name, so people are not confused as to which Fashion Week event the marketing campaign is talking about. For example, New York's Fashion Week is sponsored by Mercedes-Benz. In Toronto, the sponsor was once L'Oreal, but has since changed to World MasterCard. In other words, it was once L'Oreal Fashion Week, but now it is World MasterCard Fashion Week. To show how Mercedes-Benz Fashion Week uses the logo and brand on Facebook, I have provided an example of what the logo looks like on the original Fashion Week website.

*This is what the original Mercedes-Benz Fashion Week logo looks like. The branding is both in the Fashion Week aspect of the name, but it also combines the sponsor into the logo. It is important that*

*both names are on everything, including business cards, websites and social media profiles.*

If the sponsor was to change next year, the show would be adding a different logo and a different sponsor's name to the official look of the event's logo. It could change. However, as long as Mercedes-Benz is the sponsor for New York Fashion Week, then the logo will have to be included on everything, including social media profiles like Twitter and Facebook.

If someone decides to share a post written and published by the official Mercedes-Benz Fashion Week Facebook page, then friends of that person will be able to see that link. It is important for marketing purposes that the logo and name is present to preserve the integrity of the brand and inform new readers that the business is indeed on social media networks. Keeping the logo and name the same on all social media profiles, including blogs, isn't just for the sake of organization and appearance; it is important for the sake of branding and brand awareness. Brand awareness is all about how others see the brand in the industry, and you won't know that until the brand has made a presence in the market.

**Mercedes-Benz Fashion Week**
RUNWAY RECAP

Downtown chic for the city meets the West Coast vibe for Rebecca Minkoff Resort 2014

See it all on Style.com - > http://stylem.ag/14qa6MZ

Like · Comment · Share · 👍 68 💬 3 · 12 minutes ago · 🌐

This is a screen shot from the official Mercedes-Benz Fashion Week Facebook page. On this page, the producers of the show share snippets from the upcoming shows by providing information about upcoming designers. This one gives a sneak peek of Rebecca Minkoff's Resort Collection for 2014. As you can see, the logo with the Mercedes-Benz logo is included in the Facebook profile picture and the name of the page includes both the sponsor and the event.

You may just be starting to think about your brand. There are many components to creating a strong brand and what I have touched upon here is just the tip of a massive iceberg. Louis Vuitton didn't build the brand overnight; the logo probably came long before the client feedback about how sturdy and reliable the leather handbags were. Then, people began associating the leather goods with the logo, which then came to represent quality. Now, it is classified as one of the biggest fashion houses in the world and the quality won't disappoint. You may have to prove what you are capable of before your brand is really tested with your readers.

The best thing you can do is just create a logo that speaks to what your blog or website will be about. As the months and years go by, you may start to see yourself filling a void in the fashion industry. This void could be your branding technique. Where Louis Vuitton filled a need with leather goods and later grew bigger because of consumer demands, you could be filling a need when it comes to hair accessories. Just because the brand doesn't really stand strong now doesn't mean it won't be down the road.

# Chapter 4: Go the Business Route

Your website is now up and running with the appropriate logo and name. You know why it is important to have consistency in your branding all across the board, including on your social media profiles. At this point, you could just start publishing content and sharing it on your social media profiles in hopes of generating readership. However, if you want to start making money from your fashion blog, you must start thinking like a business person. And a business person isn't necessarily thinking about the handbags and the maxi dresses.

Since your goal is to promote the content you write on your blog, you must spend much time marketing the content. Social media marketing may only get you so much traffic, as many fashion bloggers are using the social media networks to get readers. Many Twitter accounts will have thousands of followers, but only a fraction of those followers may actually click on the link that is shared. So, if you have 100 followers, only 20 people may actually click on the link. This is why a following on Twitter or Facebook may only be so effective when it comes to marketing.

You may have to look elsewhere for marketing. As you may notice within the first week of blogging, your earnings may not be more than a few pennies or dollars as you are starting out. You have to remember that your fashion blog has no credibility with new readers and trust is something you have to earn with time. The more you see Glamour magazine, for example, the more credible and trustworthy you may find it.

You have to think like this when you are starting since you may be discouraged with the numbers you are seeing. Why would you go to another website to find fashion news when you already go to one of the most credible sources readily available online? You would go to this other site because it offers something else that isn't found on the big competitor's website, right? This is exactly the kind of thing you should be thinking about, if you want to make this fashion blog a business – and a success.

# 4.1 Online Magazines and Content Mills

If you want to make this a full-time career, you have to put in lots of effort. This means that you need to invest much time into blogging and marketing, just as a new business owner needs to invest lots of time and money into making things work. And with that said, success is not a guarantee. You can only do so much to get the readers to come. Many business owners would argue that 90% of your day should be spent marketing your website or blog.

One thing you could to spread the word about your business is to get freelance gigs on other websites in hopes of sharing links to your own website. Many content sites hire people to write about fashion and beauty, meaning you can spread the word about your name and your website. Many content-driven websites allow you to share your name, your experience and your personal website with your readers, meaning you could be sharing your website with hundreds, if not thousands, of readers.

There are plenty of content mills and online magazines online, some of which have been approved to appear in Google News. Content mills often cover many topics, ranging from gardening to automotives, home decor to fashion and so forth. Obviously, you want to apply to the fashion section, as you won't get much out of attracting technology readers, or those interested in gardening. It is all about finding your target readership.

There are plenty of content mills available, but you only want to apply to those that will allow you to share fashion-related content. Most content mills are often driven by user-submitted content and some pages pay writers a certain amount of money from the advertising clicks, depending on the traffic driven to the site.

You can apply to these sites with a resume, where you showcase your experience. You shouldn't apply with the goal of making money, but rather with the goal of finding your readers and building your credibility. You may be questioning this method, as you don't see the bigger websites using this method to draw attention to their company. However, they don't have a need to do this; they already have a trusted readership that will go directly to the website each day.

You should only see this as a temporary solution to market your blog. Once you start getting a solid readership to your website on a regular basis, you may start writing for the content mills less and less and devote more time to your website. While you write content for the other websites, you should update your blog on a regular basis to slowly grow the readership. If you have time, you should balance several websites to spread the word about your blog much faster.

# 4.2 Getting the Content and Images

As you start writing your blog, you may find yourself struggling to find both new content and usable pictures for your content. You cannot simply take pictures of a runway show from another publication and publish them on your own blog because you wrote about the show. There are copyrights on these pictures, and you could potentially get fined for taking them from one website and using them on your own website. In other words, the safest thing you can do is actually take your own pictures and use them on your website, so you don't have to worry about where you find your own pictures. If you are the kind of person who finds content by strolling through your local mall to check out the newest trends or items in stores, you could snap a few pictures here or there for your website.

The actual stories or newsworthy items you want to cover may be easy to find during busy periods, such as Fashion Week or during Awards season, but there are dry periods where nothing is happening. You should have some go-to sources for content when you experience these dry periods. Examples of places include fashion print magazines, online fashion websites, a walk through the local mall and press releases from big fashion houses or designers. You can even apply for media passes to fashion events that are happening during the fashion off-season to ensure you have something to write about. Applying for media passes is also how you get into the bigger fashion events, such as Fashion Week.

The reason why you should keep yourself in the loop is because your readers will come to expect fashion news from you. People will still read fashion news even when Fashion Week is not happening, and you should be providing that news to readers in order to build your credibility. It may take months for you to prove yourself as a professional blogger, but only the consistent bloggers will find success in this industry.

# 4.3 Understanding Monetization

Now that you have the website up and running and adding content on a daily basis, you may find yourself feeling underpaid. Welcome to the world of blogging. Many people are struggling to make ends meet with blogging, as this is very demanding and challenging profession. You will often find yourself blogging from the early morning hours until late at night with only pennies rolling in.

This is the harsh reality of blogging, which is why many people give up. The hard work isn't worth the small amounts of money coming into the bank account. The idea that running a blog involves sleeping in, going to the gym, running errands and perhaps posting two articles per day is a myth. It just doesn't happen. And the people who claim that they do so while making lots of money have probably put in the effort for many years.

With that said, it is possible to make money from your blog, especially if you are writing on a frequent basis. Making money on a blog comes down to one thing; readers. Throughout the previous chapters, I have emphasized marketing efforts, and the reason is pure and simply; the need to make money. There are several ways to make money, but all of them come down to the amount of readers you have. For example, advertisers may pay more if you can bring more readers to your blog to see the advertisements. It is all about exposure. I will touch upon fashion advertisements more in the next chapter. First, I want to introduce you to affiliate marketing, which is the easier way of running an e-commerce store.

Affiliate programs allow you to make money from sales made through your website. As a fashion blogger, you can incorporate an online shop from Amazon Associates, where you can sell items through the Amazon store. For each sale you make, you get a certain percentage. This type of income can be great if you are often doing interviews with designers that sell clothing online through Amazon. For example, Heidi Klum's clothing lines are often available on Amazon. It is a trusted online marketplace.

If you don't really blog about clothing and more about fashion events, then affiliate marketing may not be the ideal choice for you. You may have a hard time selling a dress on your blog, if you are blogging about something completely different, such as the models walking down the runway in Paris during Fashion Week.

Affiliate marketing may work well if you are representing the smaller designers who are showing collections during the local or smaller Fashion Week events. For example, don't expect Marc Jacobs to be contacting you personally and thanking you for selling his clothes on your blog. However, you could probably expect local designers to be thankful for you sharing links to their online stores. Since up-and-coming designers are often looking for exposure with their clothing lines, you could expect them to market your blog for you if you are sharing links to their clothing stores.

Keep in mind that you will only make money with the Amazon Associates if you are selling the clothing through their website. They have an HTML code you need to implement on your website, so they can track how many sales are being made through your website. You can track your earnings.

| | | | |
|---|---|---|---|
| Total Amazon.ca Items Shipped | 0 | CDN$0.00 | CDN$0.00 |
| Total Third Party Items Shipped | 0 | CDN$0.00 | CDN$0.00 |
| Total Items Shipped | 0 | CDN$0.00 | CDN$0.00 |
| Total Items Returned | 0 | CDN$0.00 | CDN$0.00 |
| Total Refunds | 0 | CDN$0.00 | CDN$0.00 |

*When you log into your Amazon Associates account, you can track items purchased, items shipped and items that have been returned to Amazon. You will also be able to see how much money you have made from the sales.*

Actual clothing falls under just one type of item you can sell through your website. You can essentially sell any type of product that falls within your niche. If you are focusing on accessories, you can sell watches, handbags, jewellery, and scarves, for example. If you are only selling handbags, you can perhaps sell some accessories including the organizational inserts that some larger handbags may benefit from, or even wallets. It is ultimately up to you what you want to sell through your website.

Alice + olivia Ophelia Lace Dress by Alice + Olivia

$495.00

Buy Now

Petunia Bell-Sleeve Dress by Alice + Olivia

$330.00

Buy Now

Alice + olivia Fierra Dress by Alice + Olivia

$198.00

Buy Now

Alice + olivia Reid Cross Back Dress by Alice + Olivia

$257.00

Buy Now

Alice + olivia Pleated Leather Miniskirt by Alice + Olivia

$396.00

Buy Now

Alice + olivia Haylie Pleated Dress by Alice + Olivia

$275.00

Buy Now

*This is what an online store would look like in the form of an affiliate program. Once the buyer clicks the "Buy Now" button, the item will be put in a shopping cart. The actual purchase happens on the affiliate's website, not your own. You are just marketing the clothing and directing the buyers to the shopping website.*

# 4.4 Advertising

Affiliate marketing is just one way to making money from your fashion blog. Many fashion stores will use online advertising programs to get the word out about their businesses and you can take advantage of their need to find a platform to share their ads. Google Adsense is one of the most successful and most reliable advertising networks out there. The Adsense program is run by Google, which means you can combine the Adsense program with any Google program, such as Google+.

Google Adsense is pretty straight forward, both in concept and in setup. Adsense takes companies that want to advertise businesses or products and places the ads on relevant websites. For example, a small clothing store in a rural area wants to spread the word about the selections available for online shopping. The store owner will invest in a marketing campaign, where they will pay a certain amount of money for certain ads. The amount of money may also influence how often the ads come up on different websites.

Google will then take these ads and find relevant websites that want to host the ads. For example, your fashion website would be an ideal place for this store to advertise on, because you are talking about clothing that could be relevant to what they are selling. Google uses keywords to help find the best sites for the ads in question. This is why your keywords on the website are so important for you in terms of ad revenue. You want to get relevant ads, not those that clearly stand out as advertisements or spam.

Because the ad program is operated by Google, there are some guidelines in place to make sure that you are respecting their service. For example, you should not spam your readers with advertisements. According to Google's terms of use, you cannot place more than three advertisement blocks on any given page. Some blocks, such as a tall sidebar or a banner across the page, may include several advertisements, meaning you could advertise as many as 15 different businesses or websites in three blocks. You can see the different ad blocks available on the Adsense website, where you can also explore different type of ads. At present time, Google offers media ads, image ads and text ads.

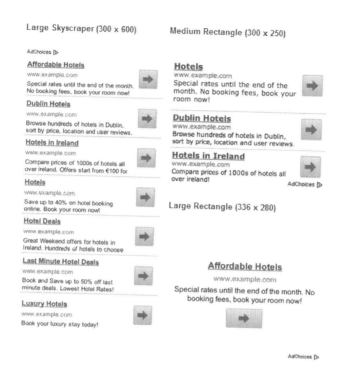

This is what text ads from Google Adsense look like. You can make sidebars like these or have the ads presented in boxes or headers that stretch horizontally across pages.

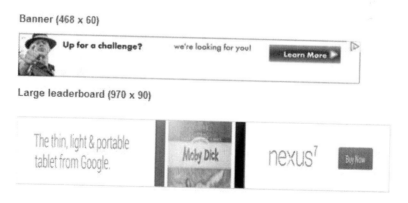

This is what image ads from Google Adsense look like. You can make sidebars like these or have the ads presented in boxes or headers that stretch horizontally across pages, just like text ads.

Medium Rectangle (300 x 250)          Large Rectangle (336 x 280)

*Video ads often come in boxes or larger layouts because of the video feature. Video ads are often called media-rich ads as well. Some videos may play automatically, while others will play when readers hover over the advertisement boxes.*

It is also simple to set up the ads on your website. After you choose the ads you want to display on your website, you will be presented with a piece of HTML code. You simply copy the code and paste it into the "Text" box of your sidebar under Widgets in Wordpress, or directly into the HTML section of the page and post section of the publishing panel. Google will then scan your website for content and keywords to find relevant ads. This process will take about 20 minutes. It is that simple.

**Estimated earnings**

**$0.00** ⑦        **$0.00**        **$0.00** ⑦        **$0.00**
Today so far      Yesterday      This month so far    Last month

**Finalized earnings** Details »

**$1.38** ⑦
Unpaid earnings
Prior to Nov 1, 2012

*This screenshot shows exactly what you see on your Adsense dashboard. You can track your earnings from a single day and the month as a whole. You can also see how much you are owed under the 'finalized earnings' section.*

# 4.5 Google News and CPM

At present time, you have a website. You know how to add content and you even have ads on your website. Now you need the readers to come your way. Of course, you can reach out to fashion lovers on various social media accounts, where you can directly target those who may be interested in the content you are sharing. However, if you are thinking about this from a business perspective, you won't be happy with 5000 viewers per month. You want to pursue upwards of 50,000 views per month and increase your income from advertisements.

While many websites will do well by getting readers through Google's search engine and social media marketing, other blogs take it one step further and apply to get included in Google News. Google News is an automated section of Google that crawl approved websites for the newest articles. The articles are then included in Google News, which is a collection of articles from top sources approved by Google. The benefit of being in Google News is the amount of readers you get. Many websites will experience tremendous growth from being included in Google News, even though it may be tough to get approved.

Google has some strict guidelines when it comes to the websites they are approving for their News service. For one, your blog must have several writers who are dedicated to writing fashion news. Some people will say that you must have a professional team of five or more, but Google decides in the end. In addition, you must make sure that you only submit news articles to Google, meaning you can't write articles, such as "How to Style a Red Dress." If the majority of your content is "how-to" articles or lists, such as "10 ways to dress for summer," then your content may not be suited for Google News. Lastly, Google has some strict technical requirements that may be tough for you to implement if you are new to web design and HTML coding.

If you are one of the lucky ones who get to include your blog in Google News, you will experience a growth of readers within days. Chances are your fashion news will be at the top of searches when people search for shows, designers or general fashion news. Once you start seeing this increase in readers, you should start thinking about larger advertising programs. While Google Adsense relies on people clicking on the ads for you to make money, CPM advertising (cost-per-thousand impressions) pays you based on how many views you have on your website. There will be a set rate based on one thousand impressions. In other words, that amount of money increases if you have thousands of readers per day.

CPM advertising allows you to make money by pulling in some larger numbers when it comes to readers. You would definitely benefit from larger advertisers, such as CPM businesses, if you are gaining thousands of readers per day. If you are interested in pursuing this type of advertising, do a simple search online to see what programs are available to you. Most of these businesses will offer ideal advertisers for your fashion website, but you have to prove a large readership to be considered.

# Chapter 5: Contracts and Copyright

As your blog grows and becomes bigger with thousands of readers finding your fashion content every day, you may find that the pressure to keep up is getting to be too much. If you are writing everything yourself, you may find it hard to take a day off because your readers are relying on you for content, and their presence on your fashion blog is your key to making money. Many larger blogs will hire writers to produce content for a percentage of the advertising revenue. These writers are hired to produce a certain amount of content, whether it is a full-time job or just a single blog post per week. Some blog owners will only pay the writers the advertising earnings generated from their own blog posts, something which can be tracked by the amount of views the content is getting. You can track this through Google Analytics by clicking on the article's page views. If the article generates 30% of all page views on the day it was published, then 30% of advertisement earnings should be paid out to the writer for that day. This is just an example. You should, of course, also track the article the following days to see if it continues to earn money.

There are no set rules when it comes to guest bloggers on your website. You can create your own rules in terms of what you expect from them and how you want to pay them. Of course, some people will write for bigger websites for free to be a part of the team or to expand their resumes, but you should not expect people to line up for you to work for free. It would be nice, but it just doesn't happen.

If you are thinking about hiring writers to write for your fashion website, even if it is on an advertising commission base, you need to protect yourself as the blog owner. At this point, you have worked hard to create a brand and get readers your way, so you don't want your writers to start ruining your standards. There are several ways you can manage writers, one of which is to take them through an extensive interview process.

You want to hire someone who is qualified to write for your blog. To make sure you find the best people, you should do interviews to make sure that the resumes reflect the people who are applying to write for your website. Everyone can write that they love fashion on a resume, but not everyone can name some big designers in the industry. If you have to, you can interview people over Skype or another online chat system, where you can hear their voices and judge their answers. Another way you can protect yourself is to give your new writers trial periods, where you edit and check their work extensively to make sure that they are not copying articles from around the web. Most importantly, you can check to see if their articles will benefit or harm your fashion brand before they are published.

If you want to stay in control of all the content you are sharing on your fashion blog, you could scan all of the work before you post it. On the other hand, you could give them access to your fashion blog and let them publish their articles on their own without your help if you trust your writers. This could save you lots of time and stress, since you don't have to guide them through everything. In addition, you could be creating a trusting bond with your writers.

Wordpress allows you to set up additional users under your administrator panel, so your new writers can easily log in to the Wordpress panel and publish articles with their own login information. Setting up a login for an individual writer is simple and can be done within minutes.

*The left-hand side Wordpress menu offers you a 'user creation' option under the 'Users' tab. Click 'Users' and select 'Add New.' Here, you can create login name and temporary password for the user. You can also administer what the user gets to see in the menu.*

Just because you create an account for a new writer doesn't mean you have to worry about exposing your entire blog to this new person. Wordpress allows you to limit the access this new writer has to your dashboard, which means that he or she cannot start editing pages, changing the code around or edit your administrative information. You can label the new writer as a "contributor," which means that the person will only have access to the writing tools on your Wordpress dashboard.

If you want to give access to a friend or someone you trust to do some editing, coding or web design, you can add the user as an administrator, which gives them access to everything. Be cautious about who you give access to, as it doesn't take much to ruin the HMTL code that makes the website functional.

Create a brand new user and add it to this site.

| | |
|---|---|
| Username *(required)* | |
| E-mail *(required)* | |
| First Name | |
| Last Name | |
| Website | |
| Password *(twice, required)* | |
| | Strength indicator     *Hint: The password sh* *numbers and symbols* |
| Send Password? | ☐ Send this password to the new user by email. |
| Role | Subscriber ▾ |
| | Subscriber |
| | Administrator |
| | Editor |
| | Author |
| | Contributor |

Add New User

*Here is a screenshot of what you have to provide in terms of information for your new user. At the bottom, you can select the role of the writer, so choose 'contributor' for your contributing writers. Click 'Add New User' when done. If you are planning on hiring an administrative assistant or manager to help you manage the magazine, give him the appropriate title in the 'role' selection and ensure he can see everything in the Wordpress menu.*

Before you create the writer's access in Wordpress, you want to make sure you protect yourself. You need to present the writer with a contract that you have crafted to protect your fashion blog and your growing brand. One bad blog post could land your brand in rough waters, so you need to make sure that the backlash falls on the author, not your fashion blog business.

# 5.1 Writer Contracts

Writer contracts are written and issued for two reasons; to create an understanding between the writer and the website in question, and to protect the website in question in regards to the content that is submitted for publication. Of course, the contract will also outline expectations and payment options, but the primary reason is to iron out the requirements for the writer. As a blog owner, you want to make sure that writers respect your brand and the efforts you have put into your fashion blog.

Since you have been building your fashion blog for months or even years at this point, you want to make sure that you outline some serious expectations. You don't want a writer to share an article that completely attacks a designer's newest collection, a designer that you happened to have a strong relationship with. A single bad article published under your brand or name could ruin some important relationships that could take you from the front row at Fashion Week to being left off the invitation list.

You may be a bit intimidated when you first start out with your contract. You can find sample contracts online, but they may not suit what you need with your fashion writers. It is therefore important that you know what you want so your contract can cover all bases. The last thing you want to do is to hire someone on one contract, only to alter it after the writer has already signed the original document.

When you start out, there are some basic questions you need to ask yourself as you draft your contract. I have divided them up below.

**Who**: You want to establish a relationship between two parties for a contract. For example, your rental contract for your apartment is between you (the person leasing the apartment) and the landlord (the person allowing you to lease the space). The same two parties should be present on the writer's contract. You should be the website owner, and the writer is the contributing person in question. Each contract should only be between two people.

**What**: You need to outline what the agreement is all about. For this part, you need to get into detail so you have the legal right to fire your writers if they don't live up to your expectations. For example, if you want them to write a certain amount of articles per week or per day, the contract needs to highlight that. The contract should also outline your expectations of how you want to communicate with them, in case you need to get a hold of your writers. Since you are running a niche website, you also need to offer a good explanation of what you expect your writers to give you at the end of the day. In return, you need to outline how you will pay them and how they will earn their money. It is only fair that your writers see the benefits in the work agreement as much as you do.

**When**: The timeline in question could be open-ended, or could be set for a certain amount of time. It all depends on what you need. For example, if you only need a writer for three months, the contract should outline this timeline. If you need a writer for a continuous period of time, then you need to clarify what needs to be done if either party needs to end the contract. For example, you as the website owner can end the contract immediately if you see fit, whereas the other party should give you some notice so you can find someone else to continue the work. Both requirements should be listed in the contract.

**Where**: Since you may be working from home, you don't want writers to stop by your apartment expecting a place to work. The "where" aspect of your contract can outline that the writers are expected to work from home and just send in their work when they are done. The location part can also refer to the part of the website where the writer will contribute articles. For example, if you run a niche website on handbags, you may have organized the site into sections by designers, news, and industry bargains.

The writer you have hired may only be responsible for contributing industry news to the site. This specification should be a part of the contract as well.

**How**: As the website owner, you may have an idea of how you want the operations to run when a writer submits articles. For example, you may trust the writer to publish on her own, so the contract should provide guidelines for obtaining a password, login information and general guidelines for getting started on your fashion blog. If you prefer to have a trial period in mind, you should outline the length of the trial period and explain your process of approving the writer. If you have any other concerns that you think your writer should know before submitting work, you should include it in the contract. It is better to have too much in your contract than too little. You don't want to confuse writers or get caught in a loop hole that could put your writers and yourself in a contractual conflict.

The contract should be presented to the writer before you give them access to your website. Make sure that the contract is signed before you actually grant writing access. Like mentioned above, you could issue the contract, wait for it to get signed and then put the writer through a trial period where you really test to see if the writer is indeed up for the job in question. Once the contract is signed, you should follow the guidelines you have put in place. It is better that you start thinking about your contract now, so you are not forced to write it the day you start getting job offers. You may forget some crucial information that could protect you down the road. You can always alter the contract between now and the time you want to hire people to make sure it suits your needs.

# 5.2 Understanding Copyright

A big part of your contract should touch upon the subject of copyright. For writers, especially those who write news-related stories and need pictures, copyright is very important. Essentially, you want to relay the message that it is not acceptable for your writers to use pictures from other websites, even though they are writing about the designer or fashion show that is hot in the news.

Copyright can be a very serious violation of the law. You may understand this if you have been writing or blogging for quite some time. I briefly revealed earlier that it would be much better if you just use pictures you have taken yourself from a fashion show or a store instead of "borrowing" pictures online. Pictures that have been published on the internet belong to someone. And that someone will do whatever in his legal power to protect his content. And you should do the same with the content you have published on your website. Make sure that people know that everything on your fashion blog is protected by copyright. You can add this statement under your "About" section or in the footer of your website.

You need to outline your copyright rules in your contract, so your writers are not stealing pictures and content from other websites in order to publish more work for more money. There are plenty of websites doing this and the sites are penalized in more ways than one. Google will penalize the sites for publishing identical content to larger sites with more credibility, and you may be receiving cease-and-desist letters from lawyers representing the sites your writers are stealing from. In the end, it is not worth it.

If the writer you are hiring is not familiar with copyright laws, it may be easier for you to simply find another writer. A simple apology for violating a copyright law may not be sufficient and could leave you with legal troubles. It is better to play it safe, than take a chance on someone who has little experience in the online publishing industry. Fashion may be a big passion of their lives, but understanding the laws should be more important.

# 5.3 Avoiding Lawsuits

Lawsuits may sound like something serious, but website owners won't hesitate to issue legal warnings or launch lawsuits if they feel that they have been violated. While you may not agree with all lawsuits filed over online issues, you would be surprised what steps website owners will take to protect their content. This includes fashion websites and journalists at Fashion Week. Stealing an article or an image will be more than enough reason for a website owner to feel violated and cause him to issue a legal warning. You want to protect yourself as a business owner and you need to take steps to ensure everything you do is original. If everything is original, you may avoid any lawsuits or legal troubles throughout your fashion blogging career.

**Images**: Whenever possible, provide the pictures you want to use for your fashion blog. It may be easier to take them off the internet, but you could be violating some serious copyright laws. If you have to take a trip to the mall once a week, or walk down your local downtown strip to get some pictures of the newest fashions, then you shouldn't hesitate to do so. And you should encourage your writers to provide their own images to protect yourself. They should provide the source so you can double-check the images, if they are indeed taken from the internet. You can always do a reverse look-up under Google Image Search to ensure that the image doesn't exist online already.

**Content**: You should always write original content. You should never copy an article online and link back to it. You may find that people have done this, but they are breaking the law and you don't want to follow suit. Plus, you have to ask yourself why your readers would want to come to your website, when everything you are offering can be found elsewhere. Lastly, it can be hard to redeem yourself with Google if they penalize your fashion blog for copying content, so you need to be on top of your original content to avoid any legal issues. To check the work from your writers, you can use various free plagiarism checkers online to ensure the work is indeed original. If the work is completely copied or scraped from another website, you should consider firing the writer immediately.

**Credits**: If you missed a Fashion Week show and you want to write about the show or designer, you could reference another article that has covered the show by being present at the event. For example, you could write, "According to New York Magazine, the show was spectacular." You then need to link to the article you are referencing to avoid any penalties. By doing this, you are also staying in the clear because you are giving credit to your source. You could, of course, offer your own interpretation of the collection or show in question, but you should credit all sources and direct quotes if you are taking them from an existing article.

# Chapter 6: Expanding Your Brand

At this point in time, you could be plenty of places with your fashion blog. Perhaps you have chosen to hire writers so you can work on your fashion blog, rather than take the actual bulk load of writing on a daily basis. Or maybe you are the one doing the actual writing on a daily basis, because you love staying in touch with everything going on in the industry, doing designer interviews and attending events whenever you can. Even though your readership may be growing on a daily basis and you feel like your website is becoming more and more popular, you should always think about growing your website, increasing your readership and expanding the brand you have been building since you first started.

While hiring writers is one way to grow your brand, you can also choose some branding methods that could increase your earnings. At this point, you are making money from your writers as you are taking a percentage of their advertising earnings on a daily basis. You are also making money from the advertisements you have throughout the site, including the home page and your own articles, whether you are using Adsense ads or have grown your readership enough to use CPM advertisements. Lastly, it is possible you have made some money from your affiliate marketing. Overall, you could be doing quite well.

However, as a blog owner, you should always think about how to expand your brand and make more money. Business owners are always thinking about lowering the costs of production, while increasing sales. You should be thinking like that, even though the latest handbags and fashion accessories should also be important; how can you increase readership and overall income from your fashion blog without increasing the number of articles you have to produce each day? Luckily, you have plenty of options when it comes to improving and expanding your brand.

# 6.1 Choosing Your Direction

Your fashion blog is one direction in itself. It is an online website that provides entertaining content and knowledge to your readers about the fashion industry, fashionable items and perhaps even designers. However, you are limited in how you are making money, how you are reaching your readers and how much you can produce in terms of quality content. To avoid becoming a content mill that simply produces content just for the sake of producing more pages with advertising you should consider expanding your brand with a more professional strategy.

It may sound nice to keep producing content in hopes of getting more ad revenue back, but Google and other search engines track the amount of content you are producing. Search engines do not support websites that mass-produce content in hopes of generating more advertising revenue. Instead, the search engines may penalize these websites by placing them lower in searches, including within Google News.

As a business owner of your fashion blog, you should be thinking about useful strategies that could increase your revenue without relying too much on search engines. Search engine traffic can only give you so much ad revenue if you want to avoid pushing your blog to the point of being categorized as a content mill. Content mills produce hundreds of articles a day, and while you can't do that on your own, your blog may fall under that category if you have many writers producing several articles per day.

You have several ways of expanding your brand, most of which can be done so with little-to-no overhead on your part. You need to think about how your brand is growing and what direction it is taking before making your brand expansion strategy. If your readers are into your blog and come on a daily basis to interact on your website, then fashionable merchandise may be a solution for brand expansion. Readers may love wearing something that pertains to your blog, if your website is very user-friendly. If your readers come for the content alone, then a magazine expansion may be the answer. It is up to you how you want to expand your brand, but I will show you some cheap methods to get what you want out of your fashion blog.

# 6.2 Low Budget Magazine Printing

When you think about starting a fashion magazine, several things may be running through your mind that is making it impossible to see this as a possibility within your tight budget. After reading this book, you may be thinking that a magazine as an impossibility without the professional pictures that you cannot get without paying for them. Second, you may be thinking about the money you have to invest in the magazine, only to have several boxes of magazines stored in your garage. Worse yet, what if the magazine doesn't sell and you have hundreds of outdated fashion magazines, which just represent your wasted money?

In today's growing business world, many companies are making it easier for business owners to take advantage of resources that would have been hundreds of dollars just years ago. HP, also known as Hewlett Packard, is one of those companies. The company is known for producing some of the best printers in the industry, so it only makes sense that the company would offer some printing options for business owners.

HP has created an online program that allows people to upload magazines created as PDF formats and print them as magazines on their high-end printers, an online program called HP MagCloud. In other words, you have to create the magazine in Word or another word processing program and save it as a PDF file. Then, you upload the singular PDF file to HP MagCloud, where you can see any changes you need to make to suit their printers. Within days, you can have a copy of your magazine in your hand. HP MagCloud will charge a certain price per page, meaning you can raise the price for the overall magazine, depending on your own profit margins. A digital version of the magazine is also offered for your own set price.

The best part of this idea is that you don't have to invest the money into getting the magazines shipped to you, only to have the responsibility of shipping it out to your readers lie on your shoulders. In fact, you don't have to have magazines stored in your home at all. HP MagCloud offers a print-on-demand service, meaning the magazines won't get printed unless someone orders a copy. It is free for you to upload your magazine file and you don't have to pay anything to make the magazine available to your readers. The only thing you have to pay for is a copy for yourself if you want it.

You have several options when it comes to your magazine and you need to think about what your fashion readers would want. One option is to sell a print magazine that offers more relevant, compelling and informative articles about the fashion industry that differ from those that appear on your blog. For example, you can share exclusive interviews with designers in your magazine, but mere commentary articles on fashion shows on your blog.

You have to think about what content people would want to pay for. In this case, the content appearing on the website is a mere introduction or teaser blog for the content in the print magazine. Don't offer the same articles on your website that are printed in the magazine. You are charging a fee for the print version, so you should offer something new and refreshing for the price.

Another option is to give your readers a free magazine, if you don't feel you can offer something new and exciting in the magazine that is worth changing money for. Even though you may not earn any income from the magazine, it is an excellent branding and marketing opportunity for your fashion blog. You are taking your fashion brand from a simple blog to a fashion empire. A print magazine does carry more credibility, because of the costs associated with running the printed magazine compared to running a website.

There are several things you have to keep in mind if you do feel like adding a magazine to your fashion brand is the way to go. For example, you need to think about the content you want to share in the magazine and how it can be worth paying money for, if that is the case. In addition, you need to plan out who will be contributing the articles for the magazine. While some of your bloggers may be interested in contributing articles, you need to make sure that you are offering something exclusive to your brand in every issue.

In addition, you have to make the magazine visually stunning. As you have already learned, there are laws in regards to taking images online for your magazine, so you may want to consider getting on press release mailing lists from fashion houses or Getty Images to make sure you are legally getting the images you want to use. You could always get an editor to edit your own pictures to make them look more professional.

Starting a magazine can be quite challenging, but the credibility your brand gets with a magazine presence is priceless. And since you can offer a magazine with little overhead on your part, it is just a matter of direction as to whether a magazine would truly suit your fashion brand.

# 6.3 Merchandise

In an earlier chapter, I told you to sell other people's clothing or fashion accessories on your blog in hopes of making a percentage of earnings from each sale. That is affiliate marketing and differs from selling merchandise on your blog. Selling merchandise as part of your brand expansion means that you would be selling your merchandise on your website. In other words, you would be selling t-shirts, tank tops, handbags and other accessories of your liking with your brand name on it. For example, how would a fashion lover like to have a Glamour Magazine tote bag? She would probably be itching to get her hands on one. As a fashion blogger, you have that option with little overhead and the strategy is similar to the magazine.

Selling merchandise on your fashion blog serves two purposes; one is to generate more income for you as a fashion business owner. While you may not make money as a fashion designer, you could make money from fashion lovers. The other is to expand your brand, as this chapter is all about brand expansion. The idea of merchandising may sound overwhelming, as you don't have the time to oversee the printing of t-shirts and you can't afford the shipping of handbags, to only have them stored in your closet because the sales aren't going as expected during the first six months. However, like the magazine, you have options of print-on-demand for merchandising as well.

You can be selective and only offer products that speak to your niche or offer a large range of products with your logo and fashion name. For example, offering a t-shirt for a man may not be applicable to your fashion blog, if you only talk about women's fashions and accessories. However, offering totes, mugs and tank tops may be more applicable to your brand, if you are targeting younger women, students, professional women and so forth.

Just a few years ago, merchandising was only done when the business truly had the profits to expand in such a manner. Designing, printing and purchasing merchandise was an expensive venture, especially because the companies had to purchase all the items and store them prior to selling them. In addition, workers had to take time to ship out the products every time a purchase was made. Luckily, you have an option that will cost you nothing. You don't even have to worry about shipping costs to your customers once a purchase is made.

Cafepress.com (or Cafepress.ca depending on your location) is a company that specializes in creating merchandise on behalf of bloggers, writers, entrepreneurs and small business owners. Cafepress offers a large variety of merchandise, including the standard t-shirts, hooded sweatshirts and mugs as well as iPhone covers, totes, aprons and baby clothing. As a fashion blog owner, you simply create an online store on the applicable Cafepress website, choose your merchandise, upload your logo and set your prices. Cafepress will have a standard printing and merchandise price, so you simply add your revenue on top of the final price to get your selling price.

You have several options when it comes to how you want to market your merchandise. One option is to simply make an advertisement on your blog that links to the store at Cafepress. Another option is to actually make a store-front display on your website by creating a brand new web-page in Wordpress, label it merchandise, and upload pictures of the products you are selling. You want to share pictures of your tote with your logo on it, rather than just the standard picture that Cafepress offers of the products you are selling.

Necklace Heart Charm
$19.99

Necklace Heart Charm
$19.99

Necklace Heart Charm
$19.99

*Jewellery is also an option for fashion blogs on Cafepress. Here is an example of necklaces, which have been customized with cupcakes. You can upload different colors to create stand-out jewellery or just sell them in the color of your logo and website.*

## Apparel

back to top

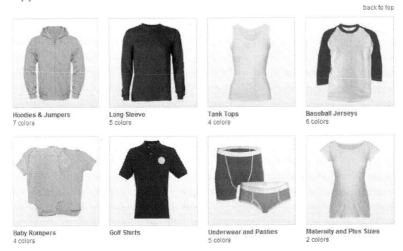

**Hoodies & Jumpers**
7 colors

**Long Sleeve**
5 colors

**Tank Tops**
4 colors

**Baseball Jerseys**
6 colors

**Baby Rompers**
4 colors

**Golf Shirts**

**Underwear and Panties**
5 colors

**Maternity and Plus Sizes**
2 colors

*This is what the selection is for shirts at Cafepress at present time. You can brand t-shirts, tank tops and even baby clothes, if you are doing a fashion niche blog on children's clothing. This is just one part of the many options available.*

You can then incorporate a "buy now" button beside the picture to prompt action. When readers click a "buy now" button, they are taken directly to your Cafepress store, where they can finish their payment. You can even link directly to the product in question, so they can simply enter their information and go straight to the check-out page on Cafepress. All of the shipping information is then provided by Cafepress. From the moment the readers make a purchase in your Cafepress store to the time the readers receive the merchandise in the mail, you do nothing but receive a royalty payment.

If you feel that this is an ideal option for you and your readers, you should do several things to make the experience a pleasant one for your readers. You should include prices and item descriptions on your blog, so your readers know what merchandise you are offering and how much it all costs. Don't make them guess – the more information you offer, the more credible your fashion blog will appear.

In addition, you should always purchase a copy of your chosen clothing to determine the quality and final product before offering the merchandise to your visitors. Your logo may not look as nice on a t-shirt as on the screen, so always test your clothing before selling it. At the end of the day, you are running a fashion blog and if your logo looks horrible on a tank top or a tote, then readers may be questioning your fashion taste.

# 6.4 Branding Expansion

No matter what direction you choose to go in when it comes to branding expansion, you have to make sure that people know about your efforts to grow your fashion blog. You can't just assume that people will notice that you have changed something on your blog, such as added a merchandise store or offering a print magazine for a purchase price.

You have to think about the expansion as a business in itself. Whether you are selling merchandise or offering a new magazine, the expansion has to be marketed in hopes of producing more readers and increase overall revenue. While you should market the expansion on your blog by creating advertising spaces in your sidebars or in article posts, you should also start spreading the word about the new products you are offering anywhere you possibly can.

If you are not currently active on social media networks, such as Facebook or Twitter, this would be an ideal time to create accounts that present your fashion blog entirely. You should not add tweets or status updates on your social media profiles about your personal life. Instead, use the social media platforms to build your brand, stay professional and share your blog articles, links to merchandise or new magazine issues.

If you are ever questioning whether you are sharing the right things on your social media profiles, you can look at some of the bigger fashion houses and see what they are sharing. For example, Glamour Magazine may share articles from the industry if they find it to applicable to their mission. In addition, Louis Vuitton may share press releases on their social media profile to spread the word about their newest product line. If you want to play like the big players in the industry, then you have to align yourself with them on the platforms where readers can be found. In other words, don't be afraid of creating a marketing strategy based on what the biggest fashion names in the industry are doing on Twitter and Facebook, for example.

Going forward, you need to think about your brand and your mission every time you make a brand expansion decision. You need to think about where you want to be in five years, what your readers want from you and what you think your brand could use to be even better. Ask yourself some crucial questions and be tough – it will only make your fashion blog better.

# Chapter 7: Organization and Accounting

If you are trying to do everything all at once that you have been taught in this book, you may feel overwhelmed. It is not a good idea to try and start a magazine or a merchandise store within your first week of running the blog. You may come across as money hungry if you have a fashion blog with ten articles about fashion designers, which are presented on a website with automated ads, a priced magazine and a large selection of merchandise. It is better to wait with the branding expansion until you have established a readership with loyal readers.

Even if you wait several months or even a year before incorporating a magazine or a merchandise store on your fashion website, you may feel overwhelmed by everything you have to remember. You have to make sure that your article posts are being published on time and on a consistent schedule. You also have to make sure that your magazine is released on time and gets promoted to your readers on social media networks. You may even think about mixing up your available merchandise on your website once or twice a year, so your readers don't get bored with your selection.

Running a fashion blog as a full-time profession isn't all about browsing for handbags online, or checking out the newest shoes in stores or in e-commerce shops. If you are planning on running your fashion blog as a full-time job, chances are that you will be spending more time marketing your platform more so than actually writing your content. If you are doing everything on your own, then you may find yourself working all the time. But if you love it, then go for it. No matter how you plan on operating your blog, you should be organized and stay up-to-date with your finances.

# 7.1 Organization

Each component of running a blog requires some serious organization to make the blog operation a smooth experience. For example, you may have a standard as to how you would like your blog posts to be written to make sure they all reach the standard you have in place for your blog. Sure, Chanel may have high standards, but you should do the same for your blog. In addition, you may have separate standards or procedures for your print magazine that you need to keep organized to ensure all issues are meeting your ideal standards. In addition, you want your magazine to have some design and layout consistencies for each issue.

Since you are possibly doing everything from your home office with a few writers from around the world, you want to make sure that you are doing everything according to your own set guidelines to ensure everything runs smoothly every day. One way to do this is to ensure all writers are using the same article structure. For example, it would be useful for search engine optimization to use the following structure: start the article with a keyword (such as Coco Chanel, or a designer's name from Fashion Week), use the keyword twice in the first 100 words and then only once per 500 words after that. You should only refer to people by the last name after introduction. Of course, if the keyword is a person's name, then simply use the name fully twice for the keyword, and then by last name throughout. This is enough for search engines to pick up on your chosen keyword. You should also include at least one outbound link, preferably to the source you are referencing. To ensure all writers are following this protocol, issue guides that explain how you want things to run.

The same doesn't have to be true for magazine standards, since your magazine issues are not being indexed in Google or other search engines. In other words, you have more freedom as to what you can do creatively in magazines. The standards you set out to your writers must also be followed by yourself. You teach others by setting great examples yourself. Every writer you hire after that should be presented with your guide book to ensure that he or she is meeting your quality standards. You want to make sure that you set the bar high, as your readers are your biggest critics.

Your personal office should also be organized, so you can find what you are looking for immediately. For example, you should print all signed contracts from writers, so you can store them all in a file folder in case you need to prove something to them. If they have crossed the line in some instances, you may need the contract immediately to prove that the writer did indeed take responsibility for the act in question by signing the contract. In addition, you may need to reference old paper work at a later date, so you don't want to waste your valuable time looking for these papers.

Lastly, you should organize your payment plans. The payment plans are not those you have for your writers, as these will be outlined in their contracts. These are ones you have to follow as the blog owner. Instead, the payment plans are the ones that tell you when you can expect to get a pay check from your Adsense account, your HP MagCloud account or your Cafepress account. You want to make sure you know when you should be getting paid, in case something goes missing in the mail or there is a technical issue on behalf of those paying you. It is always wise to be organized when you are running a professional blog, as you may not be thinking about pay checks on a daily basis.

# 7.2 Scheduling

Another organizational tip is to run your fashion blog on a schedule. For example, you may be pre-scheduling some blog posts to ensure that your readers are getting content on a regular basis even though you are not sitting in front of the computer. But you should keep track of what and when things are getting published. If possible, have a large calendar in front of you at all time that allows you to schedule posts and features for the upcoming month. You want to create a smooth balance in content, especially since Fashion Week events take place during two seasons only. You have to have content available for the slow periods, even if it means scheduling the publication for interviews a few weeks down the road.

In addition, you may have writers who are scheduling posts in advance and you should be kept in the loop about these pre-scheduled articles. If one of your writers is doing an exclusive interview with a fashion designer, you want to schedule the publication around a time that will benefit the designer. For example, if the designer is showing at an upcoming fashion show, you should publish the article a few weeks in advance to help promote the designer's name. Chances are the designer will help market the article in hopes of marketing him-or-herself.

Everything on your blog should be running smoothly. You want to make sure that you handle as many things in advance as possible, so you don't have to rush and waste valuable writing time during the week. The more organized you are, the more you will get out of running a blog. You want to be fully available in case a story breaks in the industry or a fashion designer's publicist contacts you for an interview.

# 7.3 Accounting

Of course, running a fashion blog as a business requires you to oversee many things yourself, including branding, marketing, doing the scheduling for the blog posts, scheduling interviews with designers and doing your own finances. Just because you are running your own blog and making money yourself doesn't mean you are tax-exempt. In fact, you are responsible for filing your own taxes. If you have the option, it may be a good idea to find an accountant who can handle your taxes for you, as you may be able to deduct several things, including your home office when it comes to your operational expenses. In the end, taxes need to be done.

Taxes differ in every country and sometimes, in every state, province or region. If you have never filed taxes in your hometown, you should contact someone who knows how to do it. But for yourself, you need to learn how to keep everything organized to make your accounting better for you and your fashion blog.

Create a table where you can keep track of all payments you receive, whether it is from your advertising or your merchandise account. You should write down the exact amount that goes into your bank account, the date you received it and how much the amount was. When you are calculating your earnings for the quarter or the year, you need to calculate how much money you have earned in total to figure out the tax amount owed. Depending on where you are living, you can deduct several operational expenses, which is something you should look into. You may find that you get to keep more of your tax payments after doing the deductions. While this may not have much to do with fashion writing itself, it will help you in building a solid foundation for your fashion empire.

# Conclusion

As you are wrapping up this book, you may feel you got a little more than you bargained for. Like I said in the introduction, this book is not for those who were planning on getting some help for their resumes. But those people who have picked up the book for that purpose could end up working for your fashion blog one day. At this point, I have taken you through everything you need to get started with your fashion blog. I have taught you how to start a website that gives you all of the power to truly make a custom website. I have taught you how to do brand expansion with a magazine or a merchandise store. And hopefully, I have scared you enough to not steal articles and pictures online from other sources.

Hopefully, I haven't scared you too much from the idea of running your own fashion website. Sure, it may take you a while to set up your website, to find the proper design and to write all of the content in order to just cover the home page itself. But you have to remember a few things; for one, many girls and women across the world have fashion blogs that are nowhere near yours when it comes to design. These people will use free platforms that cannot do much in terms of design and appearance. The fact that you are going after your own template to push your vision may be enough for you to stand out in a very saturated market. In addition, not many fashion bloggers have learned the importance of niche, which could give you an advantage. Most fashion bloggers write about anything and everything they like, whether it happens to be shoes, dresses, handbags, designer profiles or even fashion shows. As you have learned in this book, it can be very damaging to the success of your blog and impact the money you make.

Lastly, you don't have to do everything all at once. I have outlined things that took me years to do and teach others along the way. I have shared everything I know when it comes to growing a fashion blog over the years, so you shouldn't be too hard on yourself if you cannot see yourself doing a fashion magazine as part of your brand anytime soon. The brand expansion chapter was a mere idea to help you grow your business when you feel comfortable with your blogging experience and your content.

At this point in time, you should only think about how you will approach your blog, if you have not started anything while reading this book. You should have some kind of niche idea in mind at this point, preferably something that inspires you. You want to be one of those people who are so driven by your fashion website that you wake up in the middle of the night because you have an idea about an article or because you just want to work on your web design. Hopefully, I have given you enough tools in this book to help get you from point A to point B on your fashion venture.

If you are a planner or a control freak like me, you may feel more confident in knowing every step and every detail before actually starting with the hosting and domain registration. Many business owners will actually encourage you to draft a business plan before starting anything to ensure you cover all bases, including where the money is coming from, how much money you are investing to start your business venture and why you are doing what you are doing. In case you are that type of person, I have included a sample business plan at the end of this book in the appendix, so you can start drafting your business plan. It is the exact same business plan you can find in my book, "How to Start an Internet Business: 7 Ways to Turn Your Passion into Profit." If you can answer most of the questions in there, you are well on your way to creating a successful website. If not, simply do some research so you can complete your plan. Just because you don't have the answers now doesn't mean your fashion blog is doomed. Many businesses are developed based on the research found during the business planning process.

So, let's look at those questions I posed in the introduction. I wanted you to answer some crucial questions about whether you were truly ready to handle the big challenges of running a successful fashion blog.

**Who**: Who are you writing for on your blog? Well, part of you may think that you are writing for yourself to perhaps prove something, maybe that you are capable of this. I can tell you that you are capable. You can develop a website, create content you are passionate about, and start making money online. You shouldn't be questioning yourself at this point; you should be questioning who your target audience is based on your niche. Are you targeting the handbag lovers? Perhaps, your blog is more for the shoe lover.

**What**: In the introduction, I talked about how many people didn't know how to make a successful fashion blog. They would write anything and everything, hence a big definition of "what." However, this section should now be focusing on what you have in mind in regards to your fashion approach. Sure, you may have chosen dresses as your niche, but how are you going to talk about dresses on your blog? Perhaps, you want to try a selling approach, where each blog post has a link to an affiliate program selling a dress, where you could potentially make money. Or maybe, you only want to feature the high-end dresses.

**Where**: Hopefully, you are not questioning the "where" portion as much anymore, as I have provided you a guide to set up your website with Wordpress and your own hosting. Hopefully, you are not thinking about eBay businesses or sharing links for the sake of making money. Your mind should be flowing with ideas on how to approach your website, how to share content and where your content will be shared.

**When**: In the introduction, I addressed the proper time to start a blog. Now is the right time to start a blog. And hopefully, you have taken the time to start one as you were reading through this book. If you have not, then the right time to start a blog is now. As you have learned, it isn't so much about the first blog post when you start designing the website. You can spend weeks doing the design if you please. Just getting started is the first step. Once you see the layout and your ideas coming to life, you may be inspired and motivated to continue.

**Why**: If you cannot answer this question at this point in time, then maybe starting a fashion blog full-time is not something for you. As I have shown in this book, it can be very challenging to run a fashion blog, as you have to make sure you are there for your writers, make sure you are providing quality content to your readers, schedule trips to the mall to get your own pictures if necessary, and to make sure you stay on top of your finances. The question is; is all of this really worth it for you compared to all of the hard work you have to put in? Some people will work hard to be in control of their own business, while others prefer the 9-5 routine. So, I'll ask the same thing I did in the introduction; why would you want to be in control of your own online fashion empire and set your own schedule?

**How**: You should be able to answer this part of the conclusion. Hopefully, I have given you enough tools to get started and helped create an inspirational direction for you. When you picked up this book, you may already have had an idea in mind. I hope that this idea has only been improved with the information I have provided in this book. But hopefully, I have not crushed your dreams with the importance of niche. In fact, I hope that the information was enough to push your idea even further and has helped take your dream closer to reality.

Now that we have gone through the questions again, I hope that I have inspired you to get started. You picked up this book, because you wanted some useful information on how to start, operate and grow a fashion blog into one that stands out online. And I have shared all of my personal knowledge from writing about fashions for years, and spending hours in the front row at several Fashion Week shows. I have also tried my best to connect the world of fashion with the world of online business in hopes of giving you some confidence in pursuing whatever you want in the fashion world – at least online.

Finally, I want to share my reason for writing this book and it all comes back to the quote in the beginning - and you, the reader. I love the quote from Johann Wolfgang von Goethe - "We are shaped and fashioned by what we love" - and I love seeing people who strive to do what they are passionate about. I look forward to visiting your website and exploring your fashion empire.

# Appendix: Sample Business Plan

A well-structured business plan covers seven major aspects of starting, operating, marketing and financing a business. The seven sections include 'executive summary,' 'business description,' 'market strategies,' 'competitive analysis,' 'design and development plan,' 'operations and management plans,' and 'financial components.' You should complete each section to ensure you are on the right track and fully prepared when you launch your e-business. If you do run into problems while planning, research options to find a possible solution. Chances are that you do have several options available to make your dream website a reality.

# Executive Summary

Commonly, the 'executive summary' section follows the e-business plan's title page and should serve as a summary of everything discussed in the business plan. In other words, this single page should convey exactly what you want with the business, how you plan to obtain it and how you will finance it. Since you only have a single page to convey all of this information, you should only state the facts – not explain *how* you will use advertisements or *how* you plan to obtain guest writers. If the reader wants more information, he can reach the other sections for more detail. Although this page goes immediately after the title page, it is easier to write it after the entire plan is done, so you get all of the important information onto that single page.

# Business Description

This section is essentially a large, detailed description of what your e-business is. Is it a blog or a magazine? What services or products will be offered? For one, you want to do some research regarding the industry where your niche falls. That means you want to explore the food and wine industry for your chef's blog, or explore web design if you want to do an online community for professional designers and coders. Some of the things you must identify in the plan include:

- Are you selling a product (book, information products, etc) or are you offering a service (online community, blog with advertisements, etc)?
- Will you be manufacturing your products yourself or will you be selling them for others through affiliate programs?
- Is the business new or do you already have a brand in place?

- Are you running the business as a corporation or a sole-proprietorship? Both are business structures which must be registered with your local town or city.
- Running your e-business professionally could lead to some tax benefits
- Will you have guest contributors, online community members or will you be doing all the work yourself?
- Who are your distributors and resellers? Are you planning on selling your products on your website alone using the PayPal e-commerce system or are you planning on using Amazon's distribution channels for your self-published products, for example?
- Identify your products: what are they, how large is your product line, where will they be sold, how much will they cost to produce and what is your profit margin?
- Identify your services: what are your services, what are you planning to offer your readers for free, what services are offered for a price and what is the profit margin?

Profits are everything in any business. You cannot sell a product for the production price or any lower price, because you will be losing money and fast. In fact, it could mean that your business will be gone within months because you don't have money to pay your bills or create more production. A healthy profit margin is around 50% and anything higher is both beneficial and risky. It is beneficial for you because you get more money in your pocket, but risky because a high-priced product may not sell as well.

Create a chart that will explain how much each product or service will cost you to produce and add the profit margin. You can decide to profit margin based on your expertise or background. If you are writing books, information reports or magazines, for example, your profit margins may be set based on how much the printing and distribution costs are.

In addition, explain how your business will be profitable in comparison to other bloggers or e-businesses that are offering services or products within your industry. Use your niche angle to find a selling point that stands out and explain why people would want to choose your products over your competitors. All of this information will help you in your marketing materials and the design of your website. If you can get your selling point across quickly, you may become more successful and profitable.

# Market Strategies

This section requires you to analyze the given market you are getting into. Now, this does not mean you have to analyze the e-business market. This means you have to analyze the market your niche falls into, such as the healthy living industry, the food and wine industry, the crafting industry or the do-it-yourself industry. This is because you are getting advertisers from this industry and you will be reaching target markets within this industry. Some things you should research include:

What is the size of the market in terms of buyers? Are these markets looking for a solution you can offer with your niche products or affiliate website? Who falls into your target market? Is it busy parents, stay-at-home mothers, do-it-yourself persons, entrepreneurs, or students? Identify your target audience by narrowing down geographic location, customer attributes or product-orientation. Some products may be better suited for men than women, for example.

Identify your projecting market share: what are your distribution markets, the prices per products and your placement on the market? Will you fill a void in the market?

What are the sales potentials? Is there a demand for your products or knowledge on the market, or will your blog just add to an already saturated market?

# Competitive Analysis

As mentioned in the first chapter, it is important to research the market to determine who your competitors are before starting a niche blog or e-business. You don't want to start something that has already been done, simply adding to an industry that already has plenty of products. You may just be a small business competing with the big guys. The benefit of doing a competitor analysis is finding their flaws, so you can cash in on those. You want to fill the voids in the industries with your niche, not copy something that has been done already.

- Identify your competitors and determine their sales angle. What are they experts in? What is their niche angle? How do you differ from them? What are their sales numbers and what are their flaws? Some sales are made public, so examine where these websites or companies make the most profit
- What are your immediate competitors' strengths? Why are customers coming to them for products?

One way to identify your competitors' strengths and weaknesses is to create small profiles for each competitor. A competitor's strengths and weaknesses are usually based on the presence and absence of key assets and skills needed to compete in the market. When doing the profile, answer the following; the reasons behind successful as well as unsuccessful concepts or products, prime customer motivators, and successful products offered by the companies.

To create a competitive profile for your e-business, create comparison charts for the following; products, distribution, pricing, promotions and advertisements. In one column, describe what your competitors are doing in each area, and in a second column, identify your strategies. Find your selling points and how you are better than your competitor.

# Design and Development Plan

This section of the business plan covers anything and everything related to how the business will operate. If you are planning on operating the e-business on your own, you should still complete this section, as you need to manage everything from content to finding advertisers. There are three sections on this chapter you need to cover:

- **Product Development**: How often will you produce new products, such as books, magazines or information products? Remember, customers like reliability, so if you publish a monthly magazine, ensure the magazine is ready each month. Set a schedule that suits your daily business tasks. If you are running a niche blog, have publishing times identical each day. Use the automated publishing option, if possible.

- **Market Development**: How do you plan on spreading the word about your business? Are you planning on using SEO strategies to get your products or blog posts indexed in search engines? Do you have plans on using social media, such as Facebook and Twitter, to create a buzz about your new website? Create a marketing plan with ideas, which you can implement at different times during a single year.

- **Organizational Development**: How will the business operate on a daily basis? Are you producing everything yourself or do you have guest writers who contribute content on a daily basis? Will you have a development budget in place that allows you to hire writers after a certain income level has been reached?

# Operations and Management Plan

The operations and management section of your business plan is different from the design and development part, because operations focus on the on-going operations of the business. The development plan may describe how you plan on having writers working for you, while the operations plan will focus on how often you plan to offer work, issue payments and hire new writers. The business operations should discuss your operating expenses involved in operating the business. Of course, you have to pay for hosting and your website theme, which is a one-time cost. Hosting is a single payment once per year. Any additional domain name is around $20-$30. Any payments for writers should also be included in the operating expenses involved in the business, even if you are only getting help in researching content for your informational reports. You should also discuss how the business will operate in terms of marketing and sales, production, research and development and administration.

- **Marketing and Sales**: Create an on-going marketing plan that will explain short-term goals and long-term goals. Each marketing tactic you plan to use should have a goal of increasing sales, so make some estimates as to how much your sales level will increase. For example, a Twitter marketing campaign may sell 50 more copies of your book than your average sales. Sales and marketing go hand-in-hand. Don't forget to include income from advertisers or subscriptions
- **Production**: Production has to do with how much you plan on creating in terms of new products per month or year. Blog posts should be created more often than full-length books, for example.

Creating a production plan will help you stay on track with your publishing

- **Research and Development**: No business survives without doing some industry research, as a single industry may change drastically in a short period of time. Whether you are in the crafting industry, the do it-yourself industry or work with food, you must examine what is hot, what is trending and what people are buying. Give yourself at least a few hours per week or month to examine what is popular in your given field. One way is to use Google Alerts for keywords relevant to you, so you get emails directly to your inbox about what people are talking about and what is in demand
- **Administration**: The administration part of the business is one part that may take up much of your time, unless you are organized. Administration includes everything from getting advertisers, handling payment options for advertisers and guest writers, handling hosting and web design, controlling quality, meeting budget expectations and sending emails to new potential advertisers. If you can create a well-organized schedule, the administrative part of running a business doesn't have to take up much of your time

# Financial Components

This last part of the business plan involves creating a financial plan that works for you. The financial plan includes a functional budget that gives you some wiggle room in case you do lose some advertisers along the way, but also gives you room to grow. If you do have more than one income stream, it is a good idea to keep them separate and do financial statements at the end of the fiscal year to examine how each income stream is functioning. If you are earning the majority of profits from book sales but only mere dollars from advertising, perhaps spend more time on producing books than searching for new advertisers.

One of the things you must consider is creating income statements. In other words, these statements tell you how much you earn per product or per advertiser per month. You know exactly where the money is coming from at any given time. In addition, you can use this information to see if your marketing tactics work, as sales may increase tremendously after certain marketing campaigns. Income statements will also let you know if you are earning a big profit or losing money each month. To summarize what should go on an income statement, here is a comprehensive list from *Entrepreneur.com*.

- **Income**: Includes all the income generated by the business and its sources.
- **Cost of goods**: Includes all the costs related to the sale of products in inventory.
- **Gross profit margin**: The difference between revenue and cost of goods. Gross profit margin can be expressed in dollars, as a percentage, or both. As a percentage, the GP margin is always stated as a percentage of revenue.
- **Operating expenses**: Includes all overhead and labor expenses associated with the operations of the business.
- **Total expenses**: The sum of all overhead and labor expenses required to operate the business.
- **Net profit**: The difference between gross profit margin and total expenses, the net income depicts the business's debt and capital capabilities.
- **Depreciation**: Reflects the decrease in value of capital assets used to generate income. Also used as the basis for a tax deduction and an indicator of the flow of money into new capital.
- **Net profit before interest**: The difference between net profit and depreciation.

- **Interest**: Includes all interest derived from debts, both short-term and long-term. Interest is determined by the amount of investment within the company.
- **Net profit before taxes**: The difference between net profit before interest and interest.
- **Taxes**: Includes all taxes on the business.
- **Profit after taxes**: The difference between net profit before taxes and the taxes accrued. Profit after taxes is the bottom line for any company.

Of course, an income statement will only inform you of how much money you are pulling in each month. It doesn't necessarily tell you of how much you are spending or whether your budget is balanced. A cash flow chart will show you exactly you are spending money in as well as how much you are earning. In other words, the chart will inform you of your current financial standing at any given time.

Examples of what needs to go on a cash flow statement can be seen below in the list created by *Entrepreneur.com*.

- **Cash sales**: Income derived from sales paid for by cash.
- **Receivables**: Income derived from the collection of receivables.
- **Other income**: Income derived from investments, interest on loans that have been extended, and the liquidation of any assets.
- **Total income**: The sum of total cash, cash sales, receivables, and other income.
- **Material/merchandise**: The raw material used in the manufacture of a product (for manufacturing operations only), the cash outlay for merchandise inventory (for merchandisers such as wholesalers and retailers), or the supplies used in the performance of a service.
- **Production labor**: The labor required to manufacture a product (for manufacturing operations only) or to perform a service.

- **Overhead**: All fixed and variable expenses required for the production of the product and the operations of the business.
- **Marketing/sales**: All salaries, commissions, and other direct costs associated with the marketing and sales departments.
- **Loan payment**: The total of all payments made to reduce any long-term debts.
- **Total expenses**: The sum of material, direct labor, overhead expenses, marketing, sales, G&A, taxes, capital and loan payments.
- **Cash flow**: The difference between total income and total expenses. This amount is carried over to the next period as beginning cash.
- **Cumulative cash flow**: The difference between current cash flow and cash flow from the previous period.

Of course, not everything on this list will apply to your business, as you may not have a loan or production labor. Create your cash flow chart as it applies to your specific e-business. If you need additional support in creating your financial statements, visit *Entrepreneur.com* as this website has free resources and comprehensive articles on financial development for any kind of business.